Short Stories: 1896 to 1901

Lucy Maud Montgomery

A Case of Trespass

It was the forenoon of a hazy, breathless day, and Dan Phillips was trouting up one of the back creeks of the Carleton pond. It was somewhat cooler up the creek than out on the main body of water, for the tall birches and willows, crowding down to the brim, threw cool, green shadows across it and shut out the scorching glare, while a stray breeze now and then rippled down the wooded slopes, rustling the beech leaves with an airy, pleasant sound.

Out in the pond the glassy water creamed and shimmered in the hot sun, unrippled by the faintest breath of air. Across the soft, pearly tints of the horizon blurred the smoke of the big factory chimneys that were owned by Mr. Walters, to whom the pond and adjacent property also belonged.

Mr. Walters was a comparative stranger in Carleton, having but recently purchased the factories from the heirs of the previous owner; but he had been in charge long enough to establish a reputation for sternness and inflexibility in all his business dealings.

One or two of his employees, who had been discharged by him on what they deemed insufficient grounds, helped to deepen the impression that he was an unjust and arbitrary man, merciless to all offenders, and intolerant of the slightest infringement of his cast-iron rules.

Dan Phillips had been on the pond ever since sunrise. The trout had risen well in the early morning, but as the day wore on, growing hotter and hotter, they refused to bite, and for half an hour Dan had not caught one.

He had a goodly string of them already, however, and he surveyed them with satisfaction as he rowed his leaky little skiff to the shore of the creek.

"Pretty good catch," he soliloquized. "Best I've had this summer, so far. That big spotted one must weigh near a pound. He's a beauty. They're a good price over at the hotels now, too. I'll go home and get my dinner and go straight over with them. That'll leave me time for another try at them about sunset. Whew, how hot it is! I must take Ella May home a bunch of them blue flags. They're real handsome!"

He tied his skiff under the crowding alders, gathered a big bunch of the purple flag lilies with their silky petals, and started homeward, whistling cheerily as he stepped briskly along the fern-carpeted wood path that wound up the hill under the beeches and firs.

He was a freckled, sunburned lad of thirteen years. His neighbours all said that Danny was "as smart as a steel trap," and immediately added that they wondered where he got his smartness from—certainly not from his father!

The elder Phillips had been denominated "shiftless and slack-twisted" by all who ever had any dealings with him in his unlucky, aimless life—one of those improvident, easygoing souls who sit contentedly down to breakfast with a very faint idea where their dinner is to come from.

When he had died, no one had missed him, unless it were his patient, sad-eyed wife, who bravely faced her hard lot, and toiled unremittingly to keep a home for her two children—Dan and a girl two years younger, who was a helpless cripple, suffering from some form of spinal disease.

Dan, who was old and steady for his years, had gone manfully to work to assist his mother. Though he had been disappointed in all his efforts to obtain steady employment, he was active and obliging, and earned many a small amount by odd jobs around the village, and by helping the Carleton farmers in planting and harvest.

For the last two years, however, his most profitable source of summer income had been the trout pond. The former owner had allowed anyone who wished to fish in his pond, and Dan made a regular business of it, selling his trout at the big hotels over at Mosquito Lake. This, in spite of its unattractive name, was a popular summer resort, and Dan always found a ready market for his catch.

When Mr. Walters purchased the property it somehow never occurred to Dan that the new owner might not be so complaisant as his predecessor in the matter of the best trouting pond in the country.

To be sure, Dan often wondered why it was the pond was so deserted this summer. He could not recall having seen a single person on it save himself. Still, it did not cross his mind that there could be any particular reason for this.

He always fished up in the cool, dim creeks, which long experience had taught him were best for trout, and came and went by a convenient wood path; but he had no thought of concealment in so doing. He would not have cared had all Carleton seen him.

He had done very well with his fish so far, and prices for trout at the Lake went up every day. Dan was an enterprising boy, and a general favourite with the hotel owners. They knew that he could always be depended on.

Mrs. Phillips met him at the door when he reached home.

"See, Mother," said Dan exultantly, as he held up his fish. "Just look at that fellow, will you? A pound if he's an ounce! I ought to get a good price for these, I can tell you. Let me have my dinner now, and I'll go right over to the Lake with them."

"It's a long walk for you, Danny," replied his mother pityingly, "and it's too hot to go so far. I'm afraid you'll get sun-struck or something. You'd better wait till the cool of the evening. You're looking real pale and thin this while back."

"Oh, I'm all right, Mother," assured Dan cheerfully. "I don't mind the heat a bit. A fellow must put up with some inconveniences. Wait till I bring home the money for these fish. And I mean to have another catch tonight. It's you that's looking tired. I wish you didn't have to work so hard, Mother. If I could only get a good place you could take it easier. Sam French says that Mr. Walters wants a boy up there at the factory, but I know I wouldn't do. I ain't big enough. Perhaps something will turn up soon though. When our ship comes in, Mother, we'll have our good times."

He picked up his flags and went into the little room where his sister lay.

"See what I've brought you, Ella May!" he said, as he thrust the cool, moist clusters into her thin, eager hands. "Did you ever see such beauties?"

"Oh, Dan, how lovely they are! Thank you ever so much! If you are going over to the Lake this afternoon, will you please call at Mrs. Henny's and get those nutmeg geranium slips she promised me? Just look how nice my others are growing. The pink one is going to bloom."

"I'll bring you all the geranium slips at the Lake, if you like. When I get rich, Ella May, I'll build you a big conservatory, and I'll get every flower in the world in it for you. You shall just live and sleep among posies. Is dinner ready, Mother? Trouting's hungry work, I tell you. What paper is this?"

He picked up a folded newspaper from the table.

"Oh, that's only an old Lake Advertiser," answered Mrs. Phillips, as she placed the potatoes on the table and wiped her moist, hot face with the corner of her gingham apron. "Letty Mills brought it in around a parcel this morning. It's four weeks old, but I kept it to read if I ever get time. It's so seldom we see a paper of any kind nowadays. But I haven't looked at it yet. Why, Danny, what on earth is the matter?"

For Dan, who had opened the paper and glanced over the first page, suddenly gave a choked exclamation and turned pale, staring stupidly at the sheet before him.

"See, Mother," he gasped, as she came up in alarm and looked over his shoulder. This is what they read:

Notice

Anyone found fishing on my pond at Carleton after date will be prosecuted according to law, without respect of persons.

June First.

H.C. Walters.

"Oh, Danny, what does it mean?"

Dan went and carefully closed the door of Ella May's room before he replied. His face was pale and his voice shaky.

"Mean? Well, Mother, it just means that I've been stealing Mr. Walters's trout all summer—stealing them. That's what it means."

"Oh, Danny! But you didn't know."

"No, but I ought to have remembered that he was the new owner, and have asked him. I never thought. Mother, what does 'prosecuted according to law' mean?"

"I don't know, I'm sure, Danny. But if this is so, there's only one thing to be done. You must go straight to Mr. Walters and tell him all about it."

"Mother, I don't dare to. He is a dreadfully hard man. Sam French's father says—"

"I wouldn't believe a word Sam French's father says about Mr. Walters!" said Mrs. Phillips firmly. "He's got a spite against him because he was dismissed. Besides, Danny, it's the only right thing to do. You know that. We're poor, but we have never done anything underhand yet."

"Yes, Mother, I know," said Dan, gulping his fear bravely down. "I'll go, of course, right after dinner. I was only scared at first. I'll tell you what I'll do. I'll clean these trout nicely and take them to Mr. Walters, and tell him that, if he'll only give me time, I'll pay him back every cent of money I got for all I sold this summer. Then maybe he'll let me off, seeing as I didn't know about the notice."

"I'll go with you, Danny."

"No, I'll go alone, Mother. You needn't go with me," said Dan heroically. To himself he said that his mother had troubles enough. He would never subject her to the added ordeal of an interview with the stern factory owner. He would beard the lion in his den himself, if it had to be done.

"Don't tell Ella May anything about it. It would worry her. And don't cry, Mother, I guess it'll be all right. Let me have my dinner now and I'll go straight off."

Dan ate his dinner rapidly; then he carefully cleaned his trout, put them in a long basket, with rhubarb leaves over them, and started with an assumed cheerfulness very far from his real feelings.

He had barely passed the gate when another boy came shuffling along—a tall, raw-boned lad, with an insinuating smile and shifty, cunning eyes. The newcomer nodded familiarly to Dan.

"Hello, sonny. Going over to the Lake with your catch, are you? You'll fry up before you get there. There'll be nothing left of you but a crisp."

"No, I'm not going to the Lake. I'm going up to the factory to see Mr. Walters."

Sam French gave a long whistle of surprise.

"Why, Dan, what's taking you there? You surely ain't thinking of trying for that place, are you? Walters wouldn't look at you. Why, he wouldn't take me! You haven't the ghost of a chance."

"No, I'm not going for that. Sam, did you know that Mr. Walters had a notice in the Lake Advertiser that nobody could fish in his pond this summer?"

"Course I did—the old skinflint! He's too mean to live, that's what. He never goes near the pond himself. Regular dog in the manger, he is. Dad says —"

"Sam, why didn't you tell me about that notice?"

"Gracious, didn't you know? I s'posed everybody did, and here I've been taking you for the cutest chap this side of sunset—fishing away up in that creek where no one could see you, and cutting home through the woods on the sly. You don't mean to tell me you never saw that notice?"

"No, I didn't. Do you think I'd have gone near the pond if I had? I never saw it till today, and I'm going straight to Mr. Walters now to tell him about it."

Sam French stopped short in the dusty road and stared at Dan in undisguised amazement.

"Dan Phillips," he ejaculated, "have you plum gone out of your mind? Boy alive, you needn't be afraid that I'd peach on you. I'm too blamed glad to see anyone get the better of that old Walters, smart as he thinks himself. Gee! To dream of going to him and telling him you've been fishing in his pond! Why, he'll put you in jail. You don't know what sort of a man he is. Dad says—"

"Never mind what your dad says, Sam. My mind's made up."

"Dan, you chump, listen to me. That notice says 'prosecuted according to law.' Why, Danny, he'll put you in prison, or fine you, or something dreadful."

"I can't help it if he does," said Danny stoutly. "You get out of here, Sam French, and don't be trying to scare me. I mean to be honest, and how can I be if I don't own up to Mr. Walters that I've been stealing his trout all summer?"

"Stealing, fiddlesticks! Dan, I used to think you were a chap with some sense, but I see I was mistaken. You ain't done no harm. Walters will never miss them trout. If you're so dreadful squeamish that you won't fish no more, why, you needn't. But just let the matter drop and hold your tongue about it. That's my advice."

"Well, it isn't my mother's, then. I mean to go by hers. You needn't argue no more, Sam. I'm going."

"Go, then!" said Sam, stopping short in disgust. "You're a big fool, Dan, and serve you right if Walters lands you off to jail; but I don't wish you no ill. If I can do anything for your family after you're gone, I will, and I'll try and give your remains Christian burial—if there are any remains. So long, Danny! Give my love to old Walters!"

Dan was not greatly encouraged by this interview. He shrank more than ever from the thought of facing the stern factory owner. His courage had almost evaporated when he entered the office at the factory and asked shakily for Mr. Walters.

"He's in his office there," replied the clerk, "but he's very busy. Better leave your message with me."

"I must see Mr. Walters himself, please," said Dan firmly, but with inward trepidation.

The clerk swung himself impatiently from his stool and ushered Dan into Mr. Walters's private office.

"Boy to see you, sir," he said briefly, as he closed the ground-glass door behind him.

Dan, dizzy and trembling, stood in the dreaded presence. Mr. Walters was writing at a table covered with a businesslike litter of papers. He laid down his pen and looked up with a frown as the clerk vanished. He was a stern-looking man with deep-set grey eyes and a square, clean-shaven chin. There was not an ounce of superfluous flesh on his frame, and his voice and manner were those of the decided, resolute, masterful man of business.

He pointed to a capacious leather chair and said concisely, "What is your business with me, boy?"

Dan had carefully thought out a statement of facts beforehand, but every word had vanished from his memory. He had only a confused, desperate consciousness that he had a theft to confess and that it must be done as soon as possible. He did not sit down.

"Please, Mr. Walters," he began desperately, "I came to tell you—your notice—I never saw it before—and I've been fishing on your pond all summer—but I didn't know—honest—I've brought you all I caught today—and I'll pay back for them all—some time."

An amused, puzzled expression crossed Mr. Walters's noncommittal face. He pushed the leather chair forward.

"Sit down, my boy," he said kindly. "I don't quite understand this somewhat mixed-up statement of yours. You've been fishing on my pond, you say. Didn't you see my notice in the Advertiser?"

Dan sat down more composedly. The revelation was over and he was still alive.

"No, sir. We hardly ever see an Advertiser, and nobody told me. I'd always been used to fishing there, and I never thought but what it was all right to keep on. I know I ought to have remembered and asked you, but truly, sir, I didn't mean to steal your fish. I used to sell them over at the hotels. We saw the notice today, Mother and me, and I came right up. I've brought you the trout I caught this morning, and—if only you won't prosecute me, sir, I'll pay back every cent I got for the others—every cent, sir—if you'll give me time."

Mr. Walters passed his hand across his mouth to conceal something like a smile.

"Your name is Dan Phillips, isn't it?" he said irrelevantly, "and you live with your mother, the Widow Phillips, down there at Carleton Corners, I understand."

"Yes, sir," said Dan, wondering how Mr. Walters knew so much about him, and if these were the preliminaries of prosecution.

Mr. Walters took up his pen and drew a blank sheet towards him.

"Well, Dan, I put that notice in because I found that many people who used to fish on my pond, irrespective of leave or licence, were accustomed to lunch or camp on my property, and did not a little damage. I don't care for trouting myself; I've no time for it. However, I hardly think you'll do much damage. You can keep on fishing there. I'll give you a written permission, so that if any of my men see you they won't interfere with you. As for these trout here, I'll buy them from you at Mosquito Lake prices, and will say no more about the matter. How will that do?"

"Thank you, sir," stammered Dan. He could hardly believe his ears. He took the slip of paper Mr. Walters handed to him and rose to his feet.

"Wait a minute, Dan. How was it you came to tell me this? You might have stopped your depredations, and I should not have been any the wiser."

"That wouldn't have been honest, sir," said Dan, looking squarely at him.

There was a brief silence. Mr. Walters thrummed meditatively on the table. Dan waited wonderingly.

Finally the factory owner said abruptly, "There's a vacant place for a boy down here. I want it filled as soon as possible. Will you take it?"

"Mr. Walters! Me!" Dan thought the world must be turning upside down.

"Yes, you. You are rather young, but the duties are not hard or difficult to learn. I think you'll do. I was resolved not to fill that place until I could find a perfectly honest and trustworthy boy for it. I believe I have found him. I discharged the last boy because he lied to me about some trifling offence for which I would have forgiven him if he had told the truth. I can bear with incompetency, but falsehood and deceit I cannot and will not tolerate," he said, so sternly that Dan's face paled. "I am convinced that you are incapable of either. Will you take the place, Dan?"

"I will if you think I can fill it, sir. I will do my best."

"Yes, I believe you will. Perhaps I know more about you than you think. Businessmen must keep their eyes open. We'll regard this matter as settled then. Come up tomorrow at eight o'clock. And one word more, Dan. You have perhaps heard that I am an unjust and hard master. I am not the former, and you will never have occasion to find me the latter if you are always as truthful and straightforward as you have been today. You might easily have deceived me in this matter. That you did not do so is the best and only recommendation I require. Take those trout up to my house and leave them. That will do. Good afternoon."

Dan somehow got his dazed self through the glass door and out of the building. The whole interview had been such a surprise to him that he was hardly sure whether or not he had dreamed it all.

"I feel as if I were some person else," he said to himself, as he started down the hot white road. "But Mother was right. I'll stick to her motto. I wonder what Sam will say to this."

A Christmas Inspiration

"Well, I really think Santa Claus has been very good to us all," said Jean Lawrence, pulling the pins out of her heavy coil of fair hair and letting it ripple over her shoulders.

"So do I," said Nellie Preston as well as she could with a mouthful of chocolates. "Those blessed home folks of mine seem to have divined by instinct the very things I most wanted."

It was the dusk of Christmas Eve and they were all in Jean Lawrence's room at No. 16 Chestnut Terrace. No. 16 was a boarding-house, and boarding-houses are not proverbially cheerful places in which to spend Christmas, but Jean's room, at least, was a pleasant spot, and all the girls had brought their Christmas presents in to show each other. Christmas came on Sunday that year and the Saturday evening mail at Chestnut Terrace had been an exciting one.

Jean had lighted the pink-globed lamp on her table and the mellow light fell over merry faces as the girls chatted about their gifts. On the table was a big white box heaped with roses that betokened a bit of Christmas extravagance on somebody's part. Jean's brother had sent them to her from Montreal, and all the girls were enjoying them in common.

No. 16 Chestnut Terrace was overrun with girls generally. But just now only five were left; all the others had gone home for Christmas, but these five could not go and were bent on making the best of it.

Belle and Olive Reynolds, who were sitting on the bed—Jean could never keep them off it—were High School girls; they were said to be always laughing, and even the fact that they could not go home for Christmas because a young brother had measles did not dampen their spirits.

Beth Hamilton, who was hovering over the roses, and Nellie Preston, who was eating candy, were art students, and their homes were too far away to visit. As for Jean Lawrence, she was an orphan, and had no home of her own. She worked on the staff of one of the big city newspapers and the other girls were a little in awe of her cleverness, but her nature was a "chummy" one and her room was a favourite rendezvous. Everybody liked frank, open-handed and hearted Jean.

"It was so funny to see the postman when he came this evening," said Olive. "He just bulged with parcels. They were sticking out in every direction."

"We all got our share of them," said Jean with a sigh of content.

"Even the cook got six—I counted."

"Miss Allen didn't get a thing—not even a letter," said Beth quickly. Beth had a trick of seeing things that other girls didn't.

"I forgot Miss Allen. No, I don't believe she did," answered Jean thoughtfully as she twisted up her pretty hair. "How dismal it must be to be so forlorn as that on Christmas Eve of all times. Ugh! I'm glad I have friends."

"I saw Miss Allen watching us as we opened our parcels and letters," Beth went on. "I happened to look up once, and such an expression as was on her face, girls! It was pathetic and sad and envious all at once. It really made me feel bad—for five minutes," she concluded honestly.

"Hasn't Miss Allen any friends at all?" asked Beth.

"No, I don't think she has," answered Jean. "She has lived here for fourteen years, so Mrs. Pickrell says. Think of that, girls! Fourteen years at Chestnut Terrace! Is it any wonder that she is thin and dried-up and snappy?"

"Nobody ever comes to see her and she never goes anywhere," said Beth. "Dear me! She must feel lonely now when everybody else is being remembered by their friends. I can't forget her face tonight; it actually haunts me. Girls, how would you feel if you hadn't anyone belonging to you, and if nobody thought about you at Christmas?"

"Ow!" said Olive, as if the mere idea made her shiver.

A little silence followed. To tell the truth, none of them liked Miss Allen. They knew that she did not like them either, but considered them frivolous and pert, and complained when they made a racket.

"The skeleton at the feast," Jean called her, and certainly the presence of the pale, silent, discontented-looking woman at the No. 16 table did not tend to heighten its festivity.

Presently Jean said with a dramatic flourish, "Girls, I have an inspiration—a Christmas inspiration!"

"What is it?" cried four voices.

"Just this. Let us give Miss Allen a Christmas surprise. She has not received a single present and I'm sure she feels lonely. Just think how we would feel if we were in her place."

"That is true," said Olive thoughtfully. "Do you know, girls, this evening I went to her room with a message from Mrs. Pickrell, and I do believe she had been crying. Her room looked dreadfully bare and cheerless, too. I think she is very poor. What are we to do, Jean?"

"Let us each give her something nice. We can put the things just outside of her door so that she will see them whenever she opens it. I'll give her some of Fred's roses too, and I'll write a Christmassy letter in my very best style to go with them," said Jean, warming up to her ideas as she talked.

The other girls caught her spirit and entered into the plan with enthusiasm.

"Splendid!" cried Beth. "Jean, it is an inspiration, sure enough. Haven't we been horribly selfish—thinking of nothing but our own gifts and fun and pleasure? I really feel ashamed."

"Let us do the thing up the very best way we can," said Nellie, forgetting even her beloved chocolates in her eagerness. "The shops are open yet. Let us go up town and invest."

Five minutes later five capped and jacketed figures were scurrying up the street in the frosty, starlit December dusk. Miss Allen in her cold little room heard their gay voices and sighed. She was crying by herself in the dark. It was Christmas for everybody but her, she thought drearily.

In an hour the girls came back with their purchases.

"Now, let's hold a council of war," said Jean jubilantly. "I hadn't the faintest idea what Miss Allen would like so I just guessed wildly. I got her a lace handkerchief and a big bottle of perfume and a painted photograph frame—and I'll stick my own photo in it for fun. That was really all I could afford. Christmas purchases have left my purse dreadfully lean."

"I got her a glove-box and a pin tray," said Belle, "and Olive got her a calendar and Whittier's poems. And besides we are going to give her half of that big plummy fruit cake Mother sent us from home. I'm sure she hasn't tasted anything so delicious for years, for fruit cakes don't grow on Chestnut Terrace and she never goes anywhere else for a meal."

Beth had bought a pretty cup and saucer and said she meant to give one of her pretty water-colours too. Nellie, true to her reputation, had invested in a big box of chocolate creams, a gorgeously striped candy cane, a bag of oranges, and a brilliant lampshade of rose-coloured crepe paper to top off with.

"It makes such a lot of show for the money," she explained. "I am bankrupt, like Jean."

"Well, we've got a lot of pretty things," said Jean in a tone of satisfaction. "Now we must do them up nicely. Will you wrap them in tissue paper, girls, and tie them with baby ribbon—here's a box of it—while I write that letter?"

While the others chatted over their parcels Jean wrote her letter, and Jean could write delightful letters. She had a decided talent in that respect, and her correspondents all declared her letters to be things of beauty and joy forever. She put her best into Miss Allen's Christmas letter. Since then she has written many bright and clever things, but I do not believe she ever in her life wrote anything more genuinely original and delightful than that letter. Besides, it breathed the very spirit of Christmas, and all the girls declared that it was splendid.

"You must all sign it now," said Jean, "and I'll put it in one of those big envelopes; and, Nellie, won't you write her name on it in fancy letters?"

Which Nellie proceeded to do, and furthermore embellished the envelope by a border of chubby cherubs, dancing hand in hand around it and a sketch of No. 16 Chestnut Terrace in the corner in lieu of a stamp. Not content with this she hunted out a huge sheet of drawing paper and drew upon it an original pen-and-ink design after her own heart. A dudish cat—Miss Allen was fond of the No. 16 cat if she could be said to be fond of anything—was portrayed seated on a rocker arrayed in smoking jacket and cap with a cigar waved airily aloft in one paw while the other held out a placard bearing the legend "Merry Christmas." A second cat in full street costume bowed politely, hat in paw, and waved a banner inscribed with "Happy New Year," while faintly suggested kittens gambolled around the border. The girls laughed until they cried over it and voted it to be the best thing Nellie had yet done in original work.

All this had taken time and it was past eleven o'clock. Miss Allen had cried herself to sleep long ago and everybody else in Chestnut Terrace was abed when five figures cautiously crept down the hall, headed by Jean with a dim lamp. Outside of Miss Allen's door the procession halted and the girls silently arranged their gifts on the floor.

"That's done," whispered Jean in a tone of satisfaction as they tiptoed back. "And now let us go to bed or Mrs. Pickrell, bless her heart, will be down on us for burning so much midnight oil. Oil has gone up, you know, girls."

It was in the early morning that Miss Allen opened her door. But early as it was, another door down the hall was half open too and five rosy faces were peering cautiously out. The girls had been up for an hour for fear they would miss the sight and were all in Nellie's room, which commanded a view of Miss Allen's door.

That lady's face was a study. Amazement, incredulity, wonder, chased each other over it, succeeded by a glow of pleasure. On the floor before her was a snug little pyramid of parcels topped by Jean's letter. On a chair behind it was a bowl of delicious hot-house roses and Nellie's placard.

Miss Allen looked down the hall but saw nothing, for Jean had slammed the door just in time. Half an hour later when they were going down to breakfast Miss Allen came along the hall with outstretched hands to meet them. She had been crying again, but I think her tears were happy ones; and she was smiling now. A cluster of Jean's roses were pinned on her breast.

"Oh, girls, girls," she said, with a little tremble in her voice, "I can never thank you enough. It was so kind and sweet of you. You don't know how much good you have done me."

Breakfast was an unusually cheerful affair at No. 16 that morning. There was no skeleton at the feast and everybody was beaming. Miss Allen laughed and talked like a girl herself.

"Oh, how surprised I was!" she said. "The roses were like a bit of summer, and those cats of Nellie's were so funny and delightful. And your letter too, Jean! I cried and laughed over it. I shall read it every day for a year."

After breakfast everyone went to Christmas service. The girls went uptown to the church they attended. The city was very beautiful in the morning sunshine. There had been a white frost in the night and the tree-lined avenues and public squares seemed like glimpses of fairyland.

"How lovely the world is," said Jean.

"This is really the very happiest Christmas morning I have ever known," declared Nellie. "I never felt so really Christmassy in my inmost soul before."

"I suppose," said Beth thoughtfully, "that it is because we have discovered for ourselves the old truth that it is more blessed to give than to receive. I've always known it, in a way, but I never realized it before."

"Blessing on Jean's Christmas inspiration," said Nellie. "But, girls, let us try to make it an all-the-year-round inspiration, I say. We can bring a little of our own sunshine into Miss Allen's life as long as we live with her."

"Amen to that!" said Jean heartily. "Oh, listen, girls—the Christmas chimes!"

And over all the beautiful city was wafted the grand old message of peace on earth and good will to all the world.

A Christmas Mistake

"Tomorrow is Christmas," announced Teddy Grant exultantly, as he sat on the floor struggling manfully with a refractory bootlace that was knotted and tagless and stubbornly refused to go into the eyelets of Teddy's patched boots. "Ain't I glad, though. Hurrah!"

His mother was washing the breakfast dishes in a dreary, listless sort of way. She looked tired and broken-spirited. Ted's enthusiasm seemed to grate on her, for she answered sharply:

"Christmas, indeed. I can't see that it is anything for us to rejoice over. Other people may be glad enough, but what with winter coming on I'd sooner it was spring than Christmas. Mary Alice, do lift that child out of the ashes and put its shoes and stockings on. Everything seems to be at sixes and sevens here this morning."

Keith, the oldest boy, was coiled up on the sofa calmly working out some algebra problems, quite oblivious to the noise around him. But he looked up from his slate, with his pencil suspended above an obstinate equation, to declaim with a flourish:

"Christmas comes but once a year,

And then Mother wishes it wasn't here."

"I don't, then," said Gordon, son number two, who was preparing his own noon lunch of bread and molasses at the table, and making an atrocious mess of crumbs and sugary syrup over everything. "I know one thing to be thankful for, and that is that there'll be no school. We'll have a whole week of holidays."

Gordon was noted for his aversion to school and his affection for holidays.

"And we're going to have turkey for dinner," declared Teddy, getting up off the floor and rushing to secure his share of bread and molasses, "and cranb'ry sauce and—and—pound cake! Ain't we, Ma?"

"No, you are not," said Mrs. Grant desperately, dropping the dishcloth and snatching the baby on her knee to wipe the crust of cinders and molasses from the chubby pink-and-white face. "You may as well know it now, children, I've kept it from you so far in hopes that something would turn up, but nothing has. We can't have any Christmas dinner tomorrow—we can't afford it. I've pinched and saved every way I could for the last month, hoping that I'd be able to get a turkey for you anyhow, but you'll have to do without it. There's that doctor's bill to pay and a dozen other bills coming in—and people say they can't wait. I suppose they can't, but it's kind of hard, I must say."

The little Grants stood with open mouths and horrified eyes. No turkey for Christmas! Was the world coming to an end? Wouldn't the government interfere if anyone ventured to dispense with a Christmas celebration?

The gluttonous Teddy stuffed his fists into his eyes and lifted up his voice. Keith, who understood better than the others the look on his mother's face, took his blubbering young brother by the collar and marched him into the porch. The twins, seeing the summary proceeding, swallowed the outcries they had intended to make, although they couldn't keep a few big tears from running down their fat cheeks.

Mrs. Grant looked pityingly at the disappointed faces about her.

"Don't cry, children, you make me feel worse. We are not the only ones who will have to do without a Christmas turkey. We ought to be very thankful that we have anything to eat at all. I hate to disappoint you, but it can't be helped."

"Never mind, Mother," said Keith, comfortingly, relaxing his hold upon the porch door, whereupon it suddenly flew open and precipitated Teddy, who had been tugging at the handle, heels over head backwards. "We know you've done your best. It's been a hard year for you. Just wait, though. I'll soon be grown up, and then you and these greedy youngsters shall feast on turkey every day of the year. Hello, Teddy, have you got on your feet again? Mind, sir, no more blubbering!"

"When I'm a man," announced Teddy with dignity, "I'd just like to see you put me in the porch. And I mean to have turkey all the time and I won't give you any, either."

"All right, you greedy small boy. Only take yourself off to school now, and let us hear no more squeaks out of you. Tramp, all of you, and give Mother a chance to get her work done."

Mrs. Grant got up and fell to work at her dishes with a brighter face.

"Well, we mustn't give in; perhaps things will be better after a while. I'll make a famous bread pudding, and you can boil some molasses taffy and ask those little Smithsons next door to help you pull it. They won't whine for turkey, I'll be bound. I don't suppose they ever tasted such a thing in all their lives. If I could afford it, I'd have had them all in to dinner with us. That sermon Mr. Evans preached last Sunday kind of stirred me up. He said we ought always to try and share our Christmas joy with some poor souls who had never learned the meaning of the word. I can't do as much as I'd like to. It was different when your father was alive."

The noisy group grew silent as they always did when their father was spoken of. He had died the year before, and since his death the little family had had a hard time. Keith, to hide his feelings, began to hector the rest.

"Mary Alice, do hurry up. Here, you twin nuisances, get off to school. If you don't you'll be late and then the master will give you a whipping."

"He won't," answered the irrepressible Teddy. "He never whips us, he doesn't. He stands us on the floor sometimes, though," he added, remembering the many times his own chubby legs had been seen to better advantage on the school platform.

"That man," said Mrs. Grant, alluding to the teacher, "makes me nervous. He is the most abstracted creature I ever saw in my life. It is a wonder to me he doesn't walk straight into the river some day. You'll meet him meandering along the street, gazing into vacancy, and he'll never see you nor hear a word you say half the time."

"Yesterday," said Gordon, chuckling over the remembrance, "he came in with a big piece of paper he'd picked up on the entry floor in one hand and his hat in the other—and he stuffed his hat into the coal-scuttle and hung up the paper on a nail as grave as you please. Never knew the difference till Ned Slocum went and told him. He's always doing things like that."

Keith had collected his books and now marched his brothers and sisters off to school. Left alone with the baby, Mrs. Grant betook herself to her work with a heavy heart. But a second interruption broke the progress of her dish-washing.

"I declare," she said, with a surprised glance through the window, "if there isn't that absent-minded schoolteacher coming through the yard! What can he want? Dear me, I do hope Teddy hasn't been cutting capers in school again."

For the teacher's last call had been in October and had been occasioned by the fact that the irrepressible Teddy would persist in going to school with his pockets filled with live crickets and in driving them harnessed to strings up and down the aisle when the teacher's back was turned. All mild methods of punishment having failed, the teacher had called to talk it over with Mrs. Grant, with the happy result that Teddy's behaviour had improved—in the matter of crickets at least.

But it was about time for another outbreak. Teddy had been unnaturally good for too long a time. Poor Mrs. Grant feared that it was the calm before a storm, and it was with nervous haste that she went to the door and greeted the young teacher.

He was a slight, pale, boyish-looking fellow, with an abstracted, musing look in his large dark eyes. Mrs. Grant noticed with amusement that he wore a white straw hat in spite of the season. His eyes were directed to her face with his usual unseeing gaze.

"Just as though he was looking through me at something a thousand miles away," said Mrs. Grant afterwards. "I believe he was, too. His body was right there on the step before me, but where his soul was is more than you or I or anybody can tell."

"Good morning," he said absently. "I have just called on my way to school with a message from Miss Millar. She wants you all to come up and have Christmas dinner with her tomorrow."

"For the land's sake!" said Mrs. Grant blankly. "I don't understand." To herself she thought, "I wish I dared take him and shake him to find if he's walking in his sleep or not."

"You and all the children—every one," went on the teacher dreamily, as if he were reciting a lesson learned beforehand. "She told me to tell you to be sure and come. Shall I say that you will?"

"Oh, yes, that is—I suppose—I don't know," said Mrs. Grant incoherently. "I never expected—yes, you may tell her we'll come," she concluded abruptly.

"Thank you," said the abstracted messenger, gravely lifting his hat and looking squarely through Mrs. Grant into unknown regions. When he had gone Mrs. Grant went in and sat down, laughing in a sort of hysterical way.

"I wonder if it is all right. Could Cornelia really have told him? She must, I suppose, but it is enough to take one's breath."

Mrs. Grant and Cornelia Millar were cousins, and had once been the closest of friends, but that was years ago, before some spiteful reports and ill-natured gossip had come between them, making only a little rift at first that soon widened into a chasm of coldness and alienation. Therefore this invitation surprised Mrs. Grant greatly.

Miss Cornelia was a maiden lady of certain years, with a comfortable bank account and a handsome, old-fashioned house on the hill behind the village. She always boarded the schoolteachers and looked after them maternally; she was an active church worker and a tower of strength to struggling ministers and their families.

"If Cornelia has seen fit at last to hold out the hand of reconciliation I'm glad enough to take it. Dear knows, I've wanted to make up often enough, but I didn't think she ever would. We've both of us got too much pride and stubbornness. It's the Turner blood in us that does it. The Turners were all so set. But I mean to do my part now she has done hers."

And Mrs. Grant made a final attack on the dishes with a beaming face.

When the little Grants came home and heard the news, Teddy stood on his head to express his delight, the twins kissed each other, and Mary Alice and Gordon danced around the kitchen.

Keith thought himself too big to betray any joy over a Christmas dinner, but he whistled while doing the chores until the bare welkin in the yard rang, and Teddy, in spite of unheard of misdemeanours, was not collared off into the porch once.

When the young teacher got home from school that evening he found the yellow house full of all sorts of delectable odours. Miss Cornelia herself was concocting mince pies after the famous family recipe, while her ancient and faithful handmaiden, Hannah, was straining into moulds the cranberry jelly. The open pantry door revealed a tempting array of Christmas delicacies.

"Did you call and invite the Smithsons up to dinner as I told you?" asked Miss Cornelia anxiously.

"Yes," was the dreamy response as he glided through the kitchen and vanished into the hall.

Miss Cornelia crimped the edges of her pies delicately with a relieved air. "I made certain he'd forget it," she said. "You just have to watch him as if he were a mere child. Didn't I catch him yesterday starting off to school in his carpet slippers? And in spite of me he got away today in that ridiculous summer hat. You'd better set that jelly in the out-pantry to cool, Hannah; it looks good. We'll give those poor little Smithsons a feast for once in their lives if they never get another."

At this juncture the hall door flew open and Mr. Palmer appeared on the threshold. He seemed considerably agitated and for once his eyes had lost their look of space-searching.

"Miss Millar, I am afraid I did make a mistake this morning—it has just dawned on me. I am almost sure that I called at Mrs. Grant's and invited her and her family instead of the Smithsons. And she said they would come."

Miss Cornelia's face was a study.

"Mr. Palmer," she said, flourishing her crimping fork tragically, "do you mean to say you went and invited Linda Grant here tomorrow? Linda Grant, of all women in this world!"

"I did," said the teacher with penitent wretchedness. "It was very careless of me—I am very sorry. What can I do? I'll go down and tell them I made a mistake if you like."

"You can't do that," groaned Miss Cornelia, sitting down and wrinkling up her forehead in dire perplexity. "It would never do in the world. For pity's sake, let me think for a minute."

Miss Cornelia did think—to good purpose evidently, for her forehead smoothed out as her meditations proceeded and her face brightened. Then she got up briskly. "Well, you've done it and no mistake. I don't know that I'm sorry, either. Anyhow, we'll leave it as it is. But you must go straight down now and invite the Smithsons too. And for pity's sake, don't make any more mistakes."

When he had gone Miss Cornelia opened her heart to Hannah. "I never could have done it myself—never; the Turner is too strong in me. But I'm glad it is done. I've been wanting for years to make up with Linda. And now the chance has come, thanks to that blessed blundering boy, I mean to make the most of it. Mind, Hannah, you never whisper a word about its being a mistake. Linda must never know. Poor Linda! She's had a hard time. Hannah, we must make some more pies, and I must go straight down to the store and get some more Santa Claus stuff; I've only got enough to go around the Smithsons."

When Mrs. Grant and her family arrived at the yellow house next morning Miss Cornelia herself ran out bareheaded to meet them. The two women shook hands a little stiffly and then a rill of long-repressed affection trickled out from some secret spring in Miss Cornelia's heart and she kissed her new-found old friend tenderly. Linda returned the kiss warmly, and both felt that the old-time friendship was theirs again.

The little Smithsons all came and they and the little Grants sat down on the long bright dining room to a dinner that made history in their small lives, and was eaten over again in happy dreams for months.

How those children did eat! And how beaming Miss Cornelia and grim-faced, soft-hearted Hannah and even the absent-minded teacher himself enjoyed watching them!

After dinner Miss Cornelia distributed among the delighted little souls the presents she had bought for them, and then turned them loose in the big shining kitchen to have a taffy pull—and they had it to their hearts' content! And as for the shocking, taffyfied state into which they got their own rosy faces and that once immaculate domain—well, as Miss Cornelia and Hannah never said one word about it, neither will I.

The four women enjoyed the afternoon in their own way, and the schoolteacher buried himself in algebra to his own great satisfaction.

When her guests went home in the starlit December dusk, Miss Cornelia walked part of the way with them and had a long confidential talk with Mrs. Grant. When she returned it was to find Hannah groaning in and over the kitchen and the schoolteacher dreamily trying to clean some molasses off his boots with the kitchen hairbrush. Long-suffering Miss Cornelia rescued her property and despatched Mr. Palmer into the woodshed to find the shoe-brush. Then she sat down and laughed.

"Hannah, what will become of that boy yet? There's no counting on what he'll do next. I don't know how he'll ever get through the world, I'm sure, but I'll look after him while he's here at least. I owe him a huge debt of gratitude for this Christmas blunder. What an awful mess this place is in! But, Hannah, did you ever in the world see anything so delightful as that little Tommy Smithson stuffing himself with plum cake, not to mention Teddy Grant? It did me good just to see them."

A Strayed Allegiance

"Will you go to the Cove with me this afternoon?"

It was Marian Lesley who asked the question.

Esterbrook Elliott unpinned with a masterful touch the delicate cluster of Noisette rosebuds she wore at her throat and transferred them to his buttonhole as he answered courteously: "Certainly. My time, as you know, is entirely at your disposal."

They were standing in the garden under the creamy bloom of drooping acacia trees. One long plume of blossoms touched lightly the soft, golden-brown coils of the girl's hair and cast a wavering shadow over the beautiful, flower-like face beneath it.

Esterbrook Elliott, standing before her, thought proudly that he had never seen a woman who might compare with her. In every detail she satisfied his critical, fastidious taste. There was not a discordant touch about her.

Esterbrook Elliott had always loved Marian Lesley—or thought he had. They had grown up together from childhood. He was an only son and she an only daughter. It had always been an understood thing between the two families that the boy and girl should marry. But Marian's father had decreed that no positive pledge should pass between them until Marian was twenty-one.

Esterbrook accepted his mapped-out destiny and selected bride with the conviction that he was an exceptionally lucky fellow. Out of all the women in the world Marian was the very one whom he would have chosen as mistress of his fine, old home. She had been his boyhood's ideal. He believed that he loved her sincerely, but he was not too much in love to be blind to the worldly advantages of his marriage with his cousin.

His father had died two years previously, leaving him wealthy and independent. Marian had lost her mother in childhood; her father died when she was eighteen. Since then she had lived alone with her aunt. Her life was quiet and lonely. Esterbrook's companionship was all that brightened it, but it was enough. Marian lavished on him all the rich, womanly love of her heart. On her twenty-first birthday they were formally betrothed. They were to be married in the following autumn.

No shadow had drifted across the heaven of her happiness. She believed herself secure in her lover's unfaltering devotion. True, at times she thought his manner lacked a lover's passionate ardour. He was always attentive and courteous. She had only to utter a wish to find that it had been anticipated; he spent every spare minute at her side.

Yet sometimes she half wished he would betray more lover-like impatience and intensity. Were all lovers as calm and undemonstrative?

She reproached herself for this incipient disloyalty as often as it vexingly intruded its unwelcome presence across her inner consciousness. Surely Esterbrook was fond and devoted enough to satisfy the most exacting demands of affection. Marian herself was somewhat undemonstrative and reserved. Passing acquaintances called her cold and proud. Only the privileged few knew the rich depths of womanly tenderness in her nature.

Esterbrook thought that he fully appreciated her. As he had walked homeward the night of their betrothal, he had reviewed with unconscious criticism his mental catalogue of Marian's graces and good qualities, admitting, with supreme satisfaction, that there was not one thing about her that he could wish changed.

This afternoon, under the acacias, they had been planning about their wedding. There was no one to consult but themselves.

They were to be married early in September and then go abroad. Esterbrook mapped out the details of their bridal tour with careful thoughtfulness. They would visit all the old-world places that Marian wished to see. Afterwards they would come back home. He discussed certain changes he wished to make in the old Elliott mansion to fit it for a young and beautiful mistress.

He did most of the planning. Marian was content to listen in happy silence. Afterwards she had proposed this walk to the Cove.

"What particular object of charity have you found at the Cove now?" asked Esterbrook, with lazy interest, as they walked along.

"Mrs. Barrett's little Bessie is very ill with fever," answered Marian. Then, catching his anxious look, she hastened to add, "It is nothing infectious—some kind of a slow, sapping variety. There is no danger, Esterbrook."

"I was not afraid for myself," he replied quietly. "My alarm was for you. You are too precious to me, Marian, for me to permit you to risk health and life, if it were dangerous. What a Lady Bountiful you are to those people at the Cove. When we are married you must take me in hand and teach me your creed of charity. I'm afraid I've lived a rather selfish life. You will change all that, dear. You will make a good man of me."

"You are that now, Esterbrook," she said softly. "If you were not, I could not love you."

"It is a negative sort of goodness, I fear. I have never been tried or tempted severely. Perhaps I should fail under the test."

"I am sure you would not," answered Marian proudly.

Esterbrook laughed; her faith in him was pleasant. He had no thought but that he would prove worthy of it.

The Cove, so-called, was a little fishing hamlet situated on the low, sandy shore of a small bay. The houses, clustered in one spot, seemed like nothing so much as larger shells washed up by the sea, so grey and bleached were they from long exposure to sea winds and spray.

Dozens of ragged children were playing about them, mingled with several disreputable yellow curs that yapped noisily at the strangers.

Down on the sandy strip of beach below the houses groups of men were lounging about. The mackerel, season had not yet set in; the spring herring netting was past. It was holiday time among the sea folks. They were enjoying it to the full, a happy, ragged colony, careless of what the morrows might bring forth.

Out beyond, the boats were at anchor, floating as gracefully on the twinkling water as sea birds, their tall masts bowing landward on the swell. A lazy, dreamful calm had fallen over the distant seas; the horizon blues were pale and dim; faint purple hazes blurred the outlines of far-off headlands and cliffs; the yellow sands sparkled in the sunshine as if powdered with jewels.

A murmurous babble of life buzzed about the hamlet, pierced through by the shrill undertones of the wrangling children, most of whom had paused in their play to scan the visitors with covert curiosity.

Marian led the way to a house apart from the others at the very edge of the shelving rock. The dooryard was scrupulously clean and unlittered; the little footpath through it was neatly bordered by white clam shells; several thrifty geraniums in bloom looked out from the muslin-curtained windows.

A weary-faced woman came forward to meet them.

"Bessie's much the same, Miss Lesley," she said, in answer to Marian's inquiry. "The doctor you sent was here today and did all he could for her. He seemed quite hopeful. She don't complain or nothing—just lies there and moans. Sometimes she gets restless. It's very kind of you to come so often, Miss Lesley. Here, Magdalen, will you put this basket the lady's brought up there on the shelf?"

A girl, who had been sitting unnoticed with her back to the visitors, at the head of the child's cot in one corner of the room, stood up and slowly turned around. Marian and Esterbrook Elliott both started with involuntary surprise. Esterbrook caught his breath like a man suddenly awakened from sleep. In the name of all that was wonderful, who or what could this girl be, so little in harmony with her surroundings?

Standing in the crepuscular light of the corner, her marvellous beauty shone out with the vivid richness of some rare painting. She was tall, and the magnificent proportions of her figure were enhanced rather than marred by the severely plain dress of dark print that she wore. The heavy masses of her hair, a shining auburn dashed with golden foam, were coiled in a rich, glossy knot at the back of the classically modelled head and rippled back from a low brow whose waxen fairness even the breezes of the ocean had spared.

The girl's face was a full, perfect oval, with features of faultless regularity, and the large, full eyes were of tawny hazel, darkened into inscrutable gloom in the dimness of the corner.

Not even Marian Lesley's face was more delicately tinted, but not a trace of colour appeared in the smooth, marble-like cheeks; yet the waxen pallor bore no trace of disease or weakness, and the large, curving mouth was of an intense crimson.

She stood quite motionless. There was no trace of embarrassment or self-consciousness in her pose. When Mrs. Barrett said, "This is my niece, Magdalen Crawford," she merely inclined her head in grave, silent acknowledgement. As she moved forward to take Marian's basket, she seemed oddly out of place in the low, crowded room. Her presence seemed to throw a strange restraint over the group.

Marian rose and went over to the cot, laying her slender hand on the hot forehead of the little sufferer. The child opened its brown eyes questioningly.

"How are you today, Bessie?"

"Mad'len—I want Mad'len," moaned the little plaintive voice.

Magdalen came over and stood beside Marian Lesley.

"She wants me," she said in a low, thrilling voice; free from all harsh accent or intonation. "I am the only one she seems to know always. Yes, darling, Mad'len is here—right beside you. She will not leave you."

She knelt by the little cot and passed her arm under the child's neck, drawing the curly head close to her throat with a tender, soothing motion.

Esterbrook Elliott watched the two women intently—the one standing by the cot, arrayed in simple yet costly apparel, with her beautiful, high-bred face, and the other, kneeling on the bare, sanded floor in her print dress, with her splendid head bent low over the child and the long fringe of burnished lashes sweeping the cold pallor of the oval cheek.

From the moment that Magdalen Crawford's haunting eyes had looked straight into his for one fleeting second, an unnamable thrill of pain and pleasure stirred his heart, a thrill so strong and sudden and passionate that his face paled with emotion; the room seemed to swim before his eyes in a mist out of which gleamed that wonderful face with its mesmeric, darkly radiant eyes, burning their way into deeps and abysses of his soul hitherto unknown to him.

When the mist cleared away and his head grew steadier, he wondered at himself. Yet he trembled in every limb and the only clear idea that struggled out of his confused thoughts was an overmastering desire to take that cold face between his hands and kiss it until its passionless marble glowed into warm and throbbing life.

"Who is that girl?" he said abruptly, when they had left the cottage. "She is the most beautiful woman I have ever seen—present company always excepted," he concluded, with a depreciatory laugh.

The delicate bloom on Marian's face deepened slightly.

"You had much better to have omitted that last sentence," she said quietly, "it was so palpably an afterthought. Yes, she is wonderfully lovely—a strange beauty, I fancied. There seemed something odd and uncanny about it to me. She must be Mrs. Barrett's niece. I remember that when I was down here about a month ago Mrs. Barrett told me she expected a niece of hers to live with her —for a time at least. Her parents were both dead, the father having died recently. Mrs. Barrett seemed troubled about her. She said that the girl had been well brought up and used to better things than the Cove could give her, and she feared that she would be very discontented and unhappy. I had forgotten all about it until I saw the girl today. She certainly seems to be a very superior person; she will find the Cove very lonely, I am sure. It is not probable she will stay there long. I must see what I can do for her, but her manner seemed rather repellent, don't you think?"

"Hardly," responded Esterbrook curtly. "She seemed surprisingly dignified and self-possessed, I fancied, for a girl in her position. A princess could not have looked and bowed more royally. There was not a shadow of embarrassment in her manner, in spite of the incongruity of her surroundings. You had much better leave her alone, Marian. In all probability she would resent any condescension on your part. What wonderful, deep, lovely eyes she has."

Again the sensitive colour flushed Marian's cheek as his voice lapsed unconsciously into a dreamy, retrospective tone, and a slight restraint came over her manner, which did not depart. Esterbrook went away at sunset. Marian asked him to remain for the evening, but he pleaded some excuse.

"I shall come tomorrow afternoon," he said, as he stooped to drop a careless good-bye kiss on her face.

Marian watched him wistfully as he rode away, with an unaccountable pain in her heart. She felt more acutely than ever that there were depths in her lover's nature that she was powerless to stir into responsive life.

Had any other that power? She thought of the girl at the Cove, with her deep eyes and wonderful face. A chill of premonitory fear seized upon her.

"I feel exactly as if Esterbrook had gone away from me forever," she said slowly to herself, stooping to brush her cheek against a dew-cold, milk-white acacia bloom, "and would never come back to me again. If that could happen, I wonder what there would be left to live for?"

Esterbrook Elliott meant, or honestly thought he meant, to go home when he left Marian. Nevertheless, when he reached the road branching off to the Cove he turned his horse down it with a flush on his dark cheek. He realized that the motive of the action was disloyal to Marian and he felt ashamed of his weakness.

But the desire to see Magdalen Crawford once more and to look into the depths of her eyes was stronger than all else, and overpowered every throb of duty and resistance.

He saw nothing of her when he reached the Cove. He could think of no excuse for calling at the Barrett cottage, so he rode slowly past the hamlet and along the shore.

The sun, red as a smouldering ember, was half buried in the silken violet rim of the sea; the west was a vast lake of saffron and rose and ethereal green, through which floated the curved shallop of a thin new moon, slowly deepening from lustreless white, through gleaming silver, into burnished gold, and attended by one solitary, pearl-white star. The vast concave of sky above was of violet, infinite and flawless. Far out dusky amethystine islets clustered like gems on the shining breast of the bay. The little pools of water along the low shores glowed like mirrors of polished jacinth. The small, pine-fringed headlands ran out into the water, cutting its lustrous blue expanse like purple wedges.

As Esterbrook turned one of them he saw Magdalen standing out on the point of the next, a short distance away. Her back was towards him, and her splendid figure was outlined darkly against the vivid sky.

Esterbrook sprang from his horse and left the animal standing by itself while he walked swiftly out to her. His heart throbbed suffocatingly. He was conscious of no direct purpose save merely to see her.

She turned when he reached her with a slight start of surprise. His footsteps had made no sound on the tide-rippled sand.

For a few moments they faced each other so, eyes burning into eyes with mute soul-probing and questioning. The sun had disappeared, leaving a stain of fiery red to mark his grave; the weird, radiant light was startlingly vivid and clear. Little crisp puffs and flakes of foam scurried over the point like elfin things. The fresh wind, blowing up the bay, tossed the lustrous rings of hair about Magdalen's pale face; all the routed shadows of the hour had found refuge in her eyes.

Not a trace of colour appeared in her face under Esterbrook Elliott's burning gaze. But when he said "Magdalen!" a single, hot scorch of crimson flamed up into her cheeks protestingly. She lifted her hand with a splendid gesture, but no word passed her lips.

"Magdalen, have you nothing to say to me?" he asked, coming closer to her with an imploring passion in his face never seen by Marian Lesley's eyes. He reached out his hand, but she stepped back from his touch.

"What should I have to say to you?"

"Say that you are glad to see me."

"I am not glad to see you. You have no right to come here. But I knew you would come."

"You knew it? How?"

"Your eyes told me so today. I am not blind—I can see further than those dull fisher folks. Yes, I knew you would come. That is why I came here tonight—so that you would find me alone and I could tell you that you were not to come again."

"Why must you tell me that, Magdalen?"

"Because, as I have told you, you have no right to come."

"But if I will not obey you? If I will come in defiance of your prohibition?"

She turned her steady luminous eyes on his pale, set face.

"You would stamp yourself as a madman, then," she said coldly. "I know that you are Miss Lesley's promised husband. Therefore, you are either false to her or insulting to me. In either case the companionship of Magdalen Crawford is not what you must seek. Go!"

She turned away from him with an imperious gesture of dismissal. Esterbrook Elliott stepped forward and caught one firm, white wrist.

"I shall not obey you," he said in a low, intense tone; his fine eyes burned into hers. "You may send me away, but I will come back, again and yet again until you have learned to welcome me. Why should you meet me like an enemy? Why can we not be friends?"

The girl faced him once more.

"Because," she said proudly, "I am not your equal. There can be no friendship between us. There ought not to be. Magdalen Crawford, the fisherman's niece, is no companion for you. You will be foolish, as well as disloyal, if you ever try to see me again. Go back to the beautiful, high-bred woman you love and forget me. Perhaps you think I am talking strangely. Perhaps you think me bold and unwomanly to speak so plainly to you, a stranger. But there are some circumstances in life when plain-speaking is best. I do not want to see you again. Now, go back to your own world."

Esterbrook Elliott slowly turned from her and walked in silence back to the shore. In the shadows of the point he stopped to look back at her, standing out like some inspired prophetess against the fiery background of the sunset sky and silver-blue water. The sky overhead was thick-sown with stars; the night breeze was blowing up from its lair in distant, echoing sea caves. On his right the lights of the Cove twinkled out through the dusk.

"I feel like a coward and a traitor," he said slowly. "Good God, what is this madness that has come over me? Is this my boasted strength of manhood?"

A moment later the hoof beats of his horse died away up the shore.

Magdalen Crawford lingered on the point until the last dull red faded out into the violet gloom of the June sea dusk, than which nothing can be rarer or diviner, and listened to the moan and murmur of the sea far out over the bay with sorrowful eyes and sternly set lips.

The next day, when the afternoon sun hung hot and heavy over the water, Esterbrook Elliott came again to the Cove. He found it deserted. A rumour of mackerel had come, and every boat had sailed out in the rose-red dawn to the fishing grounds. But down on a strip of sparkling yellow sand he saw Magdalen Crawford standing, her hand on the rope that fastened a small white dory to the fragment of a half-embedded wreck.

She was watching a huddle of gulls clustered on the tip of a narrow, sandy spit running out to the left. She turned at the sound of his hurried foot-fall behind her. Her face paled slightly, and into the depths of her eyes leapt a passionate, mesmeric glow that faded as quickly as it came.

"You see I have come back in spite of your command, Magdalen."

"I do see it," she answered in a gravely troubled voice. "You are a madman who refuses to be warned."

"Where are you going, Magdalen?" She had loosened the rope from the wreck.

"I am going to row over to Chapel Point for salt. They think the boats will come in tonight loaded with mackerel—look at them away out there by the score—and salt will be needed."

"Can you row so far alone?"

"Easily. I learned to row long ago—for a pastime then. Since coming here I find it of great service to me."

She stepped lightly into the tiny shallop and picked up an oar. The brilliant sunshine streamed about her, burnishing the rich tints of her hair into ruddy gold. She balanced herself to the swaying of the dory with the grace of a sea bird. The man looking at her felt his brain reel.

"Good-bye, Mr. Elliott."

For answer he sprang into the dory and, snatching an oar, pushed against the old wreck with such energy that the dory shot out from the shore like a foam bell. His sudden spring had set it rocking violently. Magdalen almost lost her footing and caught blindly at his arm. As her fingers closed on his wrist a thrill as of fire shot through his every vein.

"Why have you done this, Mr. Elliott? You must go back."

"But I will not," he said masterfully, looking straight into her eyes with an imperiousness that sat well upon him. "I am going to row you over to Chapel Point. I have the oars—I will be master this once, at least."

For an instant her eyes flashed defiant protest, then drooped before his. A sudden, hot blush crimsoned her pale face. His will had mastered hers; the girl trembled from head to foot, and the proud, sensitive, mouth quivered.

Into the face of the man watching her breathlessly flashed a triumphant, passionate joy. He put out his hand and gently pushed her down into the seat. Sitting opposite, he took up the oars and pulled out over the sheet of sparkling blue water, through which at first the bottom of white sand glimmered wavily but afterwards deepened to translucent, dim depths of greenness.

His heart throbbed tumultuously. Once the thought of Marian drifted across his mind like a chill breath of wind, but it was forgotten when his eyes met Magdalen's.

"Tell me about yourself, Magdalen," he said at last, breaking the tremulous, charmed, sparkling silence.

"There is nothing to tell," she answered with characteristic straightforwardness. "My life has been a very uneventful one. I have never been rich, or very well educated, but—it used to be different from now. I had some chance before—before Father died."

"You must have found it very lonely and strange when you came here first."

"Yes. At first I thought I should die—but I do not mind it now. I have made friends with the sea; it has taught me a great deal. There is a kind of inspiration in the sea. When one listens to its never-ceasing murmur afar out there, always sounding at midnight and midday, one's soul goes out to meet Eternity. Sometimes it gives me so much pleasure that it is almost pain."

She stopped abruptly.

"I don't know why I am talking to you like this."

"You are a strange girl, Magdalen. Have you no other companion than the sea?"

"No. Why should I wish to have? I shall not be here long."

Elliott's face contracted with a spasm of pain.

"You are not going away, Magdalen?"

"Yes—in the fall. I have my own living to earn, you know. I am very poor. Uncle and Aunt are very kind, but I cannot consent to burden them any longer than I can help."

A sigh that was almost a moan broke from Esterbrook Elliott's lips.

"You must not go away, Magdalen. You must stay here—with me!"

"You forget yourself," she said proudly. "How dare you speak to me so? Have you forgotten Miss Lesley? Or are you a traitor to us both?"

Esterbrook made no answer. He bowed his pale, miserable face before her, self-condemned.

The breast of the bay sparkled with its countless gems like the breast of a fair woman. The shores were purple and amethystine in the distance. Far out, bluish, phantom-like sails clustered against the pallid horizon. The dory danced like a feather over the ripples. They were close under the shadow of Chapel Point.

Marian Lesley waited in vain for her lover that afternoon. When he came at last in the odorous dusk of the June night she met him on the acacia-shadowed verandah with cold sweetness. Perhaps some subtle woman-instinct whispered to her where and how he had spent the afternoon, for she offered him no kiss, nor did she ask him why he had failed to come sooner.

His eyes lingered on her in the dim light, taking in every detail of her sweet womanly refinement and loveliness, and with difficulty he choked back a groan. Again he asked himself what madness had come over him, and again for an answer rose up the vision of Magdalen Crawford's face as he had seen it that day, crimsoning beneath his gaze.

It was late when he left. Marian watched him out of sight, standing under the acacias. She shivered as with a sudden chill. "I feel as I think Vashti must have felt," she murmured aloud, "when, discrowned and unqueened, she crept out of the gates of Shushan to hide her broken heart. I wonder if Esther has already usurped my sceptre. Has that girl at the Cove, with her pale, priestess-like face and mysterious eyes, stolen his heart from me? Perhaps not, for it may never have been mine. I know that Esterbrook Elliott will be true to the letter of his vows to me, no matter what it may cost him. But I want no pallid shadow of the love that belongs to another. The hour of abdication is at hand, I fear. And what will be left for throneless Vashti then?"

Esterbrook Elliott, walking home through the mocking calm of the night, fought a hard battle with himself.

He was face to face with the truth at last—the bitter knowledge that he had never loved Marian Lesley, save with a fond, brotherly affection, and that he did love Magdalen Crawford with a passion that threatened to sweep before it every vestige of his honour and loyalty.

He had seen her but three times—and his throbbing heart lay in the hollow of her cold white hand.

He shut his eyes and groaned. What madness. What unutterable folly! He was not free—he was bound to another by every cord of honour and self-respect. And, even were he free, Magdalen Crawford would be no fit wife for him—in the eyes of the world, at least. A girl from the Cove—a girl with little education and no social standing—aye! but he loved her.

He groaned again and again in his misery. Afar down the slope the bay waters lay like an inky strip and the distant, murmurous plaint of the sea came out of the stillness of the night; the lights at the Cove glimmered faintly.

In the week that followed he went to the Cove every day. Sometimes he did not see Magdalen; at other times he did. But at the end of the week he had conquered in the bitter, heart-crushing struggle with himself. If he had weakly given way to the first mad sweep of a new passion, the strength of his manhood reasserted itself at last. Faltering and wavering were over, though there was passionate pain in his voice when he said at last, "I am not coming back again, Magdalen."

They were standing in the shadow of the pine-fringed point that ran out to the left of the Cove. They had been walking together along the shore, watching the splendour of the sea sunset that flamed and glowed in the west, where there was a sea of mackerel clouds, crimson and amber tinted, with long, ribbon-like strips of apple-green sky between. They had walked in silence, hand in hand, as children might have done, yet with the stir and throb of a mighty passion seething in their hearts.

Magdalen turned as Esterbrook spoke, and looked at him in a long silence. The bay stretched out before them, tranced and shimmering; a few stars shone down through the gloom of dusk. Right across the translucent greens and roses and blues of the west hung a dark, unsightly cloud, like the blurred outline of a monstrous bat. In the dim, reflected light the girl's mournful face took on a weird, unearthly beauty. She turned her eyes from Esterbrook Elliott's set white face to the radiant gloom of the sea.

"That is best," she answered at last, slowly.

"Best—yes! Better that we had never met! I love you—you know it—words are idle between us. I never loved before—I thought I did. I made a mistake and I must pay the penalty of that mistake. You understand me?"

"I understand," she answered simply.

"I do not excuse myself—I have been weak and cowardly and disloyal. But I have conquered myself—I will be true to the woman to whom I am pledged. You and I must not meet again. I will crush this madness to death. I think I have been delirious ever since that day I saw you first, Magdalen. My brain is clearer now. I see my duty and I mean to do it at any cost. I dare not trust myself to say more. Magdalen, I have much for which to ask your forgiveness."

"There is nothing to forgive," she said steadily. "I have been as much to blame as you. If I had been as resolute as I ought to have been—if I had sent you away the second time as I did the first—this would not have come to pass. I have been weak too, and I deserve to atone for my weakness by suffering. There is only one path open to us. Esterbrook, good-bye." Her voice quivered with an uncontrollable spasm of pain, but the misty, mournful eyes did not swerve from his. The man stepped forward and caught her in his arms.

"Magdalen, good-bye, my darling. Kiss me once—only once—before I go."

She loosened his arms and stepped back proudly.

"No! No man kisses my lips unless he is to be my husband. Good-bye, dear."

He bowed his head silently and went away, looking back not once, else he might have seen her kneeling on the damp sand weeping noiselessly and passionately.

Marian Lesley looked at his pale, determined face the next evening and read it like an open book.

She had grown paler herself; there were purple shadows under the sweet violet eyes that might have hinted of her own sleepless nights.

She greeted him calmly, holding out a steady, white hand of welcome. She saw the traces of the struggle through which he had passed and knew that he had come off victor.

The knowledge made her task a little harder. It would have been easier to let slip the straining cable than to cast it from her when it lay unresistingly in her hand.

For an instant her heart thrilled with an unutterably sweet hope. Might he not forget in time? Need she snap in twain the weakened bond between them after all? Perhaps she might win back her lost sceptre, yet if—

Womanly pride throttled the struggling hope. No divided allegiance, no hollow semblance of queenship for her!

Her opportunity came when Esterbrook asked with grave earnestness if their marriage might not be hastened a little—could he not have his bride in August? For a fleeting second Marian closed her eyes and the slender hands, lying among the laces in her lap, clasped each other convulsively.

Then she said quietly, "Sometimes I have thought, Esterbrook, that it might be better—if we were never married at all."

Esterbrook turned a startled face upon her.

"Not married at all! Marian, what do you mean?"

"Just what I say. I do not think we are as well suited to each other after all as we have fancied. We have loved each other as brother and sister might—that is all. I think it will be best to be brother and sister forever—nothing more."

Esterbrook sprang to his feet.

"Marian, do you know what you are saying? You surely cannot have heard —no one could have told you—"

"I have heard nothing," she interrupted hurriedly. "No one has told me anything. I have only said what I have been thinking of late. I am sure we have made a mistake. It is not too late to remedy it. You will not refuse my request, Esterbrook? You will set me free?"

"Good heavens, Marian!" he said hoarsely. "I cannot realize that you are in earnest. Have you ceased to care for me?" The rigidly locked hands were clasped a little tighter.

"No—I shall always care for you as my friend if you will let me. But I know we could not make each other happy—the time for that has gone by. I would never be satisfied, nor would you. Esterbrook, will you release me from a promise which has become an irksome fetter?"

He looked down on her upturned face mistily. A great joy was surging up in his heart—yet it was mingled with great regret.

He knew—none better—what was passing out of his life, what he was losing when he lost that pure, womanly nature.

"If you really mean this, Marian," he said slowly, "if you really have come to feel that your truest love is not and never can be mine—that I cannot make you happy—then there is nothing for me to do but to grant your request. You are free."

"Thank you, dear," she said gently, as she stood up.

She slipped his ring from her finger and held it out to him. He took it mechanically. He still felt dazed and unreal.

Marian held out her hand.

"Good-night, Esterbrook," she said, a little wearily. "I feel tired. I am glad you see it all in the same light as I do."

"Marian," he said earnestly, clasping the outstretched hand, "are you sure that you will be happy—are you sure that you are doing a wise thing?"

"Quite sure," she answered, with a faint smile. "I am not acting rashly. I have thought it all over carefully. Things are much better so, dear. We will always be friends. Your joys and sorrows will be to me as my own. When another love comes to bless your life, Esterbrook, I will be glad. And now, good-night. I want to be alone now."

At the doorway he turned to look back at her, standing in all her sweet stateliness in the twilight duskness, and the keen realization of all he had lost made him bow his head with a quick pang of regret.

Then he went out into the darkness of the summer night.

An hour later he stood alone on the little point where he had parted with Magdalen the night before. A restless night wind was moaning through the pines that fringed the bank behind him; the moon shone down radiantly, turning the calm expanse of the bay into a milk-white sheen.

He took Marian's ring from his pocket and kissed it reverently. Then he threw it from him far out over the water. For a second the diamond flashed in the moonlight; then, with a tiny splash, it fell among the ripples.

Esterbrook turned his face to the Cove, lying dark and silent in the curve between the crescent headlands. A solitary light glimmered from the low eaves of the Barrett cottage.

Tomorrow, was his unspoken thought, I will be free; to go back to Magdalen.

An Invitation Given on Impulse

It was a gloomy Saturday morning. The trees in the Oaklawn grounds were tossing wildly in the gusts of wind, and sodden brown leaves were blown up against the windows of the library, where a score of girls were waiting for the principal to bring the mail in.

The big room echoed with the pleasant sound of girlish voices and low laughter, for in a fortnight school would close for the holidays, and they were all talking about their plans and anticipations.

Only Ruth Mannering was, as usual, sitting by herself near one of the windows, looking out on the misty lawn. She was a pale, slender girl, with a sad face, and was dressed in rather shabby black. She had no special friend at Oaklawn, and the other girls did not know much about her. If they had thought about it at all, they would probably have decided that they did not like her; but for the most part they simply overlooked her.

This was not altogether their fault. Ruth was poor and apparently friendless, but it was not her poverty that was against her. Lou Scott, who was "as poor as a church mouse," to quote her own frank admission, was the most popular girl in the seminary, the boon companion of the richest girls, and in demand with everybody. But Lou was jolly and frank and offhanded, while Ruth was painfully shy and reserved, and that was the secret of the whole matter.

There was "no fun in her," the girls said, and so it came about that she was left out of their social life, and was almost as solitary at Oaklawn as if she had been the only girl there. She was there for the special purpose of studying music, and expected to earn her own living by teaching it when she left. She believed that the girls looked down on her on this account; this was unjust, of course, but Ruth had no idea how much her own coldness and reserve had worked against her.

Across the room Carol Golden was, as usual, the centre of an animated group; Golden Carol as her particular friends sometimes called her, partly because of her beautiful voice, and partly because of her wonderful fleece of golden hair. Carol was one of the seminary pets, and seemed to Ruth Mannering to have everything that she had not.

Presently the mail was brought in, and there was a rush to the table, followed by exclamations of satisfaction or disappointment. In a few minutes the room was almost deserted. Only two girls remained: Carol Golden, who had dropped into a big chair to read her many letters; and Ruth Mannering, who had not received any and had gone silently back to her part of the window.

Presently Carol gave a little cry of delight. Her mother had written that she might invite any friend she wished home with her to spend the holidays. Carol had asked for this permission, and now that it had come was ready to dance for joy. As to whom she would ask, there could be only one answer to that. Of course it must be her particular friend, Maud Russell, who was the cleverest and prettiest girl at Oaklawn, at least so her admirers said. She was undoubtedly the richest, and was the acknowledged "leader." The girls affectionately called her "Princess," and Carol adored her with that romantic affection that is found only among school girls. She knew, too, that Maud would surely accept her invitation because she did not intend to go home. Her parents were travelling in Europe, and she expected to spend her holidays with some cousins, who were almost strangers to her.

Carol was so much pleased that she felt as if she must talk to somebody, so she turned to Ruth.

"Isn't it delightful to think that we'll all be going home in a fortnight?"

"Yes, very—for those that have homes to go to," said Ruth drearily.

Carol felt a quick pang of pity and self-reproach. "Haven't you?" she asked.

Ruth shook her head. In spite of herself, the kindness of Carol's tone brought the tears to her eyes.

"My mother died a year ago," she said in a trembling voice, "and since then I have had no real home. We were quite alone in the world, Mother and I, and now I have nobody."

"Oh, I'm so sorry for you," cried Carol impulsively. She leaned forward and took Ruth's hand in a gentle way. "And do you mean to say that you'll have to stay here all through the holidays? Why, it will be horrid."

"Oh, I shall not mind it much," said Ruth quickly, "with study and practice most of the time. Only now, when everyone is talking about it, it makes me wish that I had some place to go."

Carol dropped Ruth's hand suddenly in the shock of a sudden idea that darted into her mind.

A stray girl passing through the hall called out, "Ruth, Miss Siviter wishes to see you about something in Room C."

Ruth got up quickly. She was glad to get away, for it seemed to her that in another minute she would break down altogether.

Carol Golden hardly noticed her departure. She gathered up her letters and went abstractedly to her room, unheeding a gay call for "Golden Carol" from a group of girls in the corridor. Maud Russell was not in and Carol was glad. She wanted to be alone and fight down that sudden idea.

"It is ridiculous to think of it," she said aloud, with a petulance very unusual in Golden Carol, whose disposition was as sunny as her looks. "Why, I simply cannot. I have always been longing to ask Maud to visit me, and now that the chance has come I am not going to throw it away. I am very sorry for Ruth, of course. It must be dreadful to be all alone like that. But it isn't my fault. And she is so fearfully quiet and dowdy—what would they all think of her at home? Frank and Jack would make such fun of her. I shall ask Maud just as soon as she comes in."

Maud did come in presently, but Carol did not give her the invitation. Instead, she was almost snappish to her idol, and the Princess soon went out again in something of a huff.

"Oh, dear," cried Carol, "now I've offended her. What has got into me? What a disagreeable thing a conscience is, although I'm sure I don't know why mine should be prodding me so! I don't want to invite Ruth Mannering home with me for the holidays, but I feel exactly as if I should not have a minute's peace of mind all the time if I didn't. Mother would think it all right, of course. She would not mind if Ruth dressed in calico and never said anything but yes and no. But how the boys would laugh! I simply won't do it, conscience or no conscience."

In view of this decision it was rather strange that the next morning, Carol Golden went down to Ruth Mannering's lonely little room on Corridor Two and said, "Ruth, will you go home with me for the holidays? Mother wrote me to invite anyone I wished to. Don't say you can't come, dear, because you must."

Carol never, as long as she lived, forgot Ruth's face at that moment.

"It was absolutely transfigured," she said afterwards. "I never saw anyone look so happy in my life."

A fortnight later unwonted silence reigned at Oaklawn. The girls were scattered far and wide, and Ruth Mannering and Carol Golden were at the latter's home.

Carol was a very much surprised girl. Under the influence of kindness and pleasure Ruth seemed transformed into a different person. Her shyness and reserve melted away in the sunny atmosphere of the Golden home. Mrs. Golden took her into her motherly heart at once; and as for Frank and Jack, whose verdict Carol had so dreaded, they voted Ruth "splendid." She certainly got along very well with them; and if she did not make the social sensation that pretty Maud Russell might have made, the Goldens all liked her and Carol was content.

"Just four days more," sighed Carol one afternoon, "and then we must go back to Oaklawn. Can you realize it, Ruth?"

Ruth looked up from her book with a smile. Even in appearance she had changed. There was a faint pink in her cheeks and a merry light in her eyes.

"I shall not be sorry to go back to work," she said. "I feel just like it because I have had so pleasant a time here that it has heartened me up for next term. I think it will be very different from last. I begin to see that I kept to myself too much and brooded over fancied slights."

"And then you are to room with me since Maud is not coming back," said Carol. "What fun we shall have. Did you ever toast marshmallows over the gas? Why, I declare, there is Mr. Swift coming up the walk. Look, Ruth! He is the richest man in Westleigh."

Ruth peeped out of the window over Carol's shoulder.

"He reminds me of somebody," she said absently, "but I can't think who it is. Of course, I have never seen him before. What a good face he has!"

"He is as good as he looks," said Carol, enthusiastically. "Next to Father, Mr. Swift is the nicest man in the world. I have always been quite a pet of his. His wife is dead, and so is his only daughter. She was a lovely girl and died only two years ago. It nearly broke Mr. Swift's heart. And he has lived alone ever since in that great big house up at the head of Warner Street, the one you admired so, Ruth, the last time we were uptown. There's the bell for the second time, Mary can't have heard it. I'll go myself."

As Carol showed the caller into the room, Ruth rose to leave and thus came face to face with him. Mr. Swift started perceptibly.

"Mr. Swift, this is my school friend, Miss Mannering," said Carol.

Mr. Swift seemed strangely agitated as he took Ruth's timidly offered hand.

"My dear young lady," he said hurriedly, "I am going to ask you what may seem a very strange question. What was your mother's name?"

"Agnes Hastings," answered Ruth in surprise. And then Carol really thought that Mr. Swift had gone crazy, for he drew Ruth into his arms and kissed her.

"I knew it," he said. "I was sure you were Agnes' daughter, for you are the living image of what she was when I last saw her. Child, you don't know me, but I am your Uncle Robert. Your mother was my half-sister."

"Oh, Mr. Swift!" cried Carol, and then she ran for her mother.

Ruth turned pale and dropped into a chair, and Mr. Swift sat down beside her.

"To think that I have found you at last, child. How puzzled you look. Did your mother never speak of me? How is she? Where is she?"

"Mother died last year," said Ruth.

"Poor Agnes! And I never knew! Don't cry, little girl. I want you to tell me all about it. She was much younger than I was, and when our mother died my stepfather went away and took her with him. I remained with my father's people and eventually lost all trace of my sister. I was a poor boy then, but things have looked up with me and I have often tried to find her."

By this time Carol had returned with her father and mother, and there was a scene—laughing, crying, explaining—and I don't really know which of the two girls was the more excited, Carol or Ruth. As for Mr. Swift, he was overjoyed to find his niece and wanted to carry her off with him then and there, but Mrs. Golden insisted on her finishing her visit. When the question of returning to Oaklawn came up, Mr. Swift would not hear of it at first, but finally yielded to Carol's entreaties and Ruth's own desire.

"I shall graduate next year, Uncle, and then I can come back to you for good."

That evening when Ruth was alone in her room, trying to collect her thoughts and realize that the home and love that she had so craved were really to be hers at last, Golden Carol was with her mother in the room below, talking it all over.

"Just think, Mother, if I had not asked Ruth to come here, this would not have happened. And I didn't want to, I wanted to ask Maud so much, and I was dreadfully disappointed when I couldn't—for I really couldn't. I could not help remembering the look in Ruth's eyes when she said that she had no home to go to, and so I asked her instead of Maud. How dreadful it would have been if I hadn't."

Detected by the Camera

One summer I was attacked by the craze for amateur photography. It became chronic afterwards, and I and my camera have never since been parted. We have had some odd adventures together, and one of the most novel of our experiences was that in which we played the part of chief witness against Ned Brooke.

I may say that my name is Amy Clarke, and that I believe I am considered the best amateur photographer in our part of the country. That is all I need tell you about myself.

Mr. Carroll had asked me to photograph his place for him when the apple orchards were in bloom. He has a picturesque old-fashioned country house behind a lawn of the most delightful old trees and flanked on each side by the orchards. So I went one June afternoon, with all my accoutrements, prepared to "take" the Carroll establishment in my best style.

Mr. Carroll was away but was expected home soon, so we waited for him, as all the family wished to be photographed under the big maple at the front door. I prowled around among the shrubbery at the lower end of the lawn and, after a great deal of squinting from various angles, I at last fixed upon the spot from which I thought the best view of the house might be obtained. Then Gertie and Lilian Carroll and I got into the hammocks and swung at our leisure, enjoying the cool breeze sweeping through the maples.

Ned Brooke was hanging around as usual, watching us furtively. Ned was one of the hopeful members of a family that lived in a tumble-down shanty just across the road from the Carrolls. They were wretchedly poor, and old Brooke, as he was called, and Ned were employed a good deal by Mr. Carroll —more out of charity than anything else, I fancy.

The Brookes had a rather shady reputation. They were notoriously lazy, and it was suspected that their line of distinction between their own and their neighbours' goods was not very clearly drawn. Many people censured Mr. Carroll for encouraging them at all, but he was too kind-hearted to let them suffer actual want and, as a consequence, one or the other of them was always dodging about his place.

Ned was a lank, tow-headed youth of about fourteen, with shifty, twinkling eyes that could never look you straight in the face. His appearance was anything but prepossessing, and I always felt, when I looked at him, that if anyone wanted to do a piece of shady work by proxy, Ned Brooke would be the very lad for the business.

Mr. Carroll came at last, and we all went down to meet him at the gate.

Ned Brooke also came shuffling along to take the horse, and Mr. Carroll tossed the reins to him and at the same time handed a pocketbook to his wife.

"Just as well to be careful where you put that," he said laughingly. "There's a sum in it not to be picked up on every gooseberry bush. Gilman Harris paid me this morning for that bit of woodland I sold him last fall—five hundred dollars. I promised that you and the girls should have it to get a new piano, so there it is for you."

"Thank you," said Mrs. Carroll delightedly. "However, you'd better put it back in your pocket till we go in. Amy is in a hurry."

Mr. Carroll took back the pocketbook and dropped it carelessly into the inside pocket of the light overcoat that he wore.

I happened to glance at Ned Brooke just then, and I could not help noticing the sudden crafty, eager expression that flashed over his face. He eyed the pocketbook in Mr. Carroll's hands furtively, after which he went off with the horse in a great hurry.

The girls were exclaiming and thanking their father, and nobody noticed Ned Brooke's behaviour but myself, and it soon passed out of my mind.

"Come to take the place, are you, Amy?" said Mr. Carroll. "Well, everything is ready, I think. I suppose we'd better proceed. Where shall we stand? You had better group us as you think best."

Whereupon I proceeded to arrange them in due order under the maple. Mrs. Carroll sat in a chair, while her husband stood behind her. Gertie stood on the steps with a basket of flowers in her hand, and Lilian was at one side. The two little boys, Teddy and Jack, climbed up into the maple, and little Dora, the dimpled six-year-old, stood gravely in the foreground with an enormous grey cat hugged in her chubby arms.

It was a pretty group in a pretty setting, and I thrilled with professional pride as I stepped back for a final, knowing squint at it all. Then I went to my camera, slipped in the plate, gave them due warning and took off the cap.

I took two plates to make sure and then the thing was over, but as I had another plate left I thought I might as well take a view of the house by itself, so I carried my camera to a new place and had just got everything ready to lift the cap when Mr. Carroll came down and said:

"If you girls want to see something pretty, come to the back field with me. That will wait till you come back, won't it, Amy?"

So we all betook ourselves to the back field, a short distance away, where Mr. Carroll proudly displayed two of the prettiest little Jersey cows I had ever seen.

We returned to the house by way of the back lane and, as we came in sight of the main road, my brother Cecil drove up and said that if I were ready, I had better go home with him and save myself a hot, dusty walk.

The Carrolls all went down to the fence to speak to Cecil, but I dashed hurriedly down through the orchard, leaped over the fence into the lawn and ran to the somewhat remote corner where I had left my camera. I was in a desperate hurry, for I knew Cecil's horse did not like to be kept waiting, so I never even glanced at the house, but snatched off the cap, counted two and replaced it.

Then I took out my plate, put it in the holder and gathered up my traps. I suppose I was about five minutes at it all and I had my back to the house the whole time, and when I laid all my things ready and emerged from my retreat, there was nobody to be seen about the place.

As I hurried up through the lawn, I noticed Ned Brooke walking at a smart pace down the lane, but the fact did not make any particular impression on me at the time, and was not recalled until afterwards.

Cecil was waiting for me, so I got in the buggy and we drove off. On arriving home I shut myself up in my dark room and proceeded to develop the first two negatives of the Carroll housestead. They were both excellent, the first one being a trifle the better, so that I decided to finish from it. I intended also to develop the third, but just as I finished the others, a half-dozen city cousins swooped down upon us and I had to put away my paraphernalia, emerge from my dark retreat and fly around to entertain them.

The next day Cecil came in and said:

"Did you hear, Amy, that Mr. Carroll has lost a pocketbook with five hundred dollars in it?"

"No!" I exclaimed. "How? When? Where?"

"Don't overwhelm a fellow. I can answer only one question—last night. As to the 'how,' they don't know, and as to the 'where'—well, if they knew that, there might be some hope of finding it. The girls are in a bad way. The money was to get them their longed-for piano, it seems, and now it's gone."

"But how did it happen, Cecil?"

"Well, Mr. Carroll says that Mrs. Carroll handed the pocketbook back to him at the gate yesterday, and he dropped it in the inside pocket of his overcoat—"

"I saw him do it," I cried.

"Yes, and then, before he went to be photographed, he hung his coat up in the hall. It hung there until the evening, and nobody seems to have thought about the money, each supposing that someone else had put it carefully away. After tea Mr. Carroll put on the coat and went to see somebody over at Netherby. He says the thought of the pocketbook never crossed his mind; he had forgotten all about putting it in that coat pocket. He came home across the fields about eleven o'clock and found that the cows had broken into the clover hay, and he had a great chase before he got them out. When he went in, just as he entered the door, the remembrance of the money flashed over him. He felt in his pocket, but there was no pocketbook there; he asked his wife if she had taken it out. She had not, and nobody else had. There was a hole in the pocket, but Mr. Carroll says it was too small for the pocketbook to have worked through. However, it must have done so—unless someone took it out of his pocket at Netherby, and that is not possible, because he never had his coat off, and it was in an inside pocket. It's not likely that they will ever see it again. Someone may pick it up, of course, but the chances are slim. Mr. Carroll doesn't know his exact path across the fields, and if he lost it while he was after the cows, it's a bluer show still. They've been searching all day, of course. The girls are awfully disappointed."

A sudden recollection came to me of Ned Brooke's face as I had seen it the day before at the gate, coupled with the remembrance of seeing him walking down the lane at a quick pace, so unlike his usual shambling gait, while I ran through the lawn.

"How do they know it was lost?" I said. "Perhaps it was stolen before Mr. Carroll went to Netherby."

"They think not," said Cecil. "Who would have stolen it?"

"Ned Brooke. I saw him hanging around. And you never saw such a look as came over his face when he heard Mr. Carroll say there was five hundred dollars in that pocketbook."

"Well, I did suggest to them that Ned might know something about it, for I remembered having seen him go down the lane while I was waiting for you, but they won't hear of such a thing. The Brookes are kind of protégés of theirs, you know, and they won't believe anything bad of them. If Ned did take it, however, there's not a shadow of evidence against him."

"No, I suppose not," I answered thoughtfully, "but the more I think it over, the more I'm convinced that he took it. You know, we all went to the back field to look at the Jerseys, and all that time the coat was hanging there in the hall, and not a soul in the house. And it was just after we came back that I saw Ned scuttling down the lane so fast."

I mentioned my suspicions to the Carrolls a few days afterwards, when I went down with the photographs, and found that they had discovered no trace of the lost pocketbook. But they seemed positively angry when I hinted that Ned Brooke might know more about its whereabouts than anyone else. They declared that they would as soon think of suspecting one of themselves as Ned, and altogether they seemed so offended at my suggestion that I held my peace and didn't irritate them by any more suppositions.

Afterwards, in the excitement of our cousins' visit, the matter passed out of my mind completely. They stayed two weeks, and I was so busy the whole time that I never got a chance to develop that third plate and, in fact, I had forgotten all about it.

One morning soon after they went away, I remembered the plate and decided to go and develop it. Cecil went with me, and we shut ourselves up in our den, lit our ruby lantern and began operations. I did not expect much of the plate, because it had been exposed and handled carelessly, and I thought that it might prove to be underexposed or light-struck. So I left Cecil to develop it while I prepared the fixing bath. Cecil was whistling away when suddenly he gave a tremendous "whew" of astonishment and sprang to his feet.

"Amy, Amy, look here!" he cried.

I rushed to his side and looked at the plate as he held it up in the rosy light. It was a splendid one, and the Carroll house came out clear, with the front door and the steps in full view.

And there, just in the act of stepping from the threshold, was the figure of a boy with an old straw hat on his head and—in his hand—the pocketbook!

He was standing with his head turned towards the corner of the house as if listening, with one hand holding his ragged coat open and the other poised in mid-air with the pocketbook, as if he were just going to put it in his inside pocket. The whole scene was as clear as noonday, and nobody with eyes in his head could have failed to recognize Ned Brooke.

"Goodness!" I gasped. "In with it—quick!"

And we doused the thing into the fixing bath and then sat down breathlessly and looked at each other.

"I say, Amy," said Cecil, "what a sell this will be on the Carrolls! Ned Brooke couldn't do such a thing—oh, no! The poor injured boy at whom everyone has such an unlawful pick! I wonder if this will convince them."

"Do you think they can get it all back?" I asked. "It's not likely he would have dared to use any of it yet."

"I don't know. We'll have a try, anyhow. How long before this plate will be dry enough to carry down to the Carrolls as circumstantial evidence?"

"Three hours or thereabouts," I answered, "but perhaps sooner. I'll take two prints off when it is ready. I wonder what the Carrolls will say."

"It's a piece of pure luck that the plate should have turned out so well after the slap-dash way in which it was taken and used. I say, Amy, isn't this quite an adventure?"

At last the plate was dry, and I printed two proofs. We wrapped them up carefully and marched down to Mr. Carroll's.

You never saw people so overcome with astonishment as the Carrolls were when Cecil, with the air of a statesman unfolding the evidence of some dreadful conspiracy against the peace and welfare of the nation, produced the plate and the proofs, and held them out before them.

Mr. Carroll and Cecil took the proofs and went over to the Brooke shanty. They found only Ned and his mother at home. At first Ned, when taxed with his guilt, denied it, but when Mr. Carroll confronted him with the proofs, he broke down in a spasm of terror and confessed all. His mother produced the pocketbook and the money—they had not dared to spend a single cent of it— and Mr. Carroll went home in triumph.

Perhaps Ned Brooke ought not to have been let off so easily as he was, but his mother cried and pleaded, and Mr. Carroll was too kind-hearted to resist. So he did not punish them at all, save by utterly discarding the whole family and their concerns. The place got too hot for them after the story came out, and in less than a month all moved away—much to the benefit of Mapleton.

In Spite of Myself

My trunk was packed and I had arranged with my senior partner—I was the junior member of a law firm—for a month's vacation. Aunt Lucy had written that her husband had gone on a sea trip and she wished me to superintend the business of his farm and mills in his absence, if I could arrange to do so. She added that "Gussie" thought it was a pity to trouble me, and wanted to do the overseeing herself, but that she—Aunt Lucy—preferred to have a man at the head of affairs.

I had never seen my step-cousin, Augusta Ashley, but I knew, from Aunt Lucy's remarks concerning her, pretty much what sort of person she was—just the precise kind I disliked immeasurably. I had no idea what her age was, but doubtless she was over thirty, tall, determined, aggressive, with a "faculty" for managing, a sharp, probing nose, and a y-formation between her eyebrows. I knew the type, and I was assured that the period of sojourn with my respected aunt would be one of strife between Miss Ashley and myself.

I wrote to Aunt Lucy to expect me, made all necessary arrangements, and went to bid Nellie goodbye. I had made up my mind to marry Nellie. I had never openly avowed myself her suitor, but we were cousins, and had grown up together, so that I knew her well enough to be sure of my ground. I liked her so well that it was easy to persuade myself that I was in love with her. She more nearly fulfilled the requirements of my ideal wife than anyone I knew. She was pleasant to look upon, without being distractingly pretty; small and fair and womanly. She dressed nicely, sang and played agreeably, danced well, and had a cheerful, affectionate disposition. She was not alarmingly clever, had no "hobbies," and looked up to me as heir to all the wisdom of the ages—what man does not like to be thought clever and brilliant? I had no formidable rival, and our families were anxious for the match. I considered myself a lucky fellow. I felt that I would be very lonely without Nellie when I was away, and she admitted frankly that she would miss me awfully. She looked so sweet that I was on the point of asking her then and there to marry me. Well, fate interfered in the guise of a small brother, so I said goodbye and left, mentally comparing her to my idea of Miss Augusta Ashley, much to the latter's disadvantage.

When I stepped from the train at a sleepy country station next day I was promptly waylaid by a black-eyed urchin who informed me that Mrs. Ashley had sent him with an express wagon for my luggage, and that "Miss Gussie" was waiting with the carriage at the store, pointing down to a small building before whose door a girl was trying to soothe her frightened horse.

As I went down the slope towards her I noticed she was tall—quite too tall for my taste. I dislike women who can look into my eyes on a level—but I had to admit that her form was remarkably symmetrical and graceful. She put out her hand—it was ungloved and large, but white and firm, with a cool, pleasant touch—and said, with a composure akin to indifference, "Mr. Carslake, I presume. Mother could not come to meet you, so she sent me. Will you be kind enough to hold my horse for a few minutes? I want to get something in the store." Whereupon she calmly transferred the reins to me and disappeared.

At the time she certainly did not impress me as pretty, yet neither could I call her plain. Taken separately, her features were good. Her nose was large and straight, the mouth also a trifle large but firm and red, the brow wide and white, shadowed by a straying dash of brown curl or two. She had a certain cool, statuesque paleness, accentuated by straight, fine, black brows, and her eyes were a bluish grey; but the pupils, as I afterward found out, had a trick of dilating into wells of blackness which, added to a long fringe of very dark lashes, made her eyes quite the most striking feature of her face. Her expression was open and frank, and her voice clear and musical without being sweet. She looked about twenty-two.

At the time I did not fancy her appearance and made a mental note to the effect that I would never like Miss Ashley. I had no use for cool, businesslike women—women should have no concern with business. Nellie would never have troubled her dear, curly head over it.

Miss Ashley came out with her arms full of packages, stowed them away in the carriage, got in, told me which road to take, and did not again speak till we were out of the village and driving along a pretty country lane, arched over with crimson maples and golden-brown beeches. The purplish haze of a sunny autumn day mellowed over the fields, and the bunch of golden rod at my companion's belt was akin to the plumed ranks along the fences. I hazarded the remark that it was a fine day; Miss Ashley gravely admitted that it was. Then a deep smile seemed to rise somewhere in her eyes and creep over her face, discovering a dimple here and there as it proceeded.

"Don't let's talk about the weather—the subject is rather stale," she said. "I suppose you are wondering why on earth Mother had to drag you away out here. I tried to show her how foolish it was, but I didn't succeed. Mother thinks there must be a man at the head of affairs or they'll never go right. I could have taken full charge easily enough; I haven't been Father's 'boy' all my life for nothing. There was no need to take you away from your business."

I protested. I said I was going to take a vacation anyway, and business was not pressing just then. I also hinted that, while I had no doubt of her capacity, she might have found the duties of superintendent rather arduous.

"Not at all," she said, with a serenity that made me groan inwardly. "I like it. Father always said I was a born business manager. You'll find Ashley's Mills very quiet, I'm afraid. It's a sort of charmed Sleepy Hollow. See, there's home," as we turned a maple-blazoned corner and looked from the crest of one hill across to that of another. "Home" was a big, white, green-shuttered house buried amid a riot of autumn colour, with a big grove of dark green spruces at the back. Below them was a glimpse of a dark blue mill pond and beyond it long sweeps of golden-brown meadow land, sloping up till they dimmed in horizon mists of pearl and purple.

"How pretty," I exclaimed admiringly.

"Isn't it?" said Gussie proudly. "I love it." Her pupils dilated into dark pools, and I rather unwillingly admitted that Miss Ashley was a fine-looking girl.

As we drove up Aunt Lucy was standing on the steps of the verandah, over whose white roof trailed a luxuriant creeper, its leaves tinged by October frosts into lovely wine reds and tawny yellows. Gussie sprang out, barely touching my offered hand with her fingertips.

"There's Mother waiting to pounce on you and hear all the family news," she said, "so go and greet her like a dutiful nephew."

"I must take out your horse for you first," I said politely.

"Not at all," said Miss Ashley, taking the reins from my hands in a way not to be disputed. "I always unharness Charley myself. No one understands him half so well. Besides, I'm used to it. Didn't I tell you I'd always been Father's boy?"

"I well believe it," I thought in disgust, as she led the horse over to the well and I went up to Aunt Lucy. Through the sitting-room windows I kept a watchful eye on Miss Ashley as she watered and deftly unharnessed Charley and led him into his stable with sundry pats on his nose. Then I saw no more of her till she came in to tell us tea was ready, and led the way out to the dining room.

It was evident Miss Gussie held the reins of household government, and no doubt worthily. Those firm, capable white hands of hers looked as though they might be equal to a good many emergencies. She talked little, leaving the conversation to Aunt Lucy and myself, though she occasionally dropped in an apt word. Toward the end of the meal, however, she caught hold of an unfortunate opinion I had incautiously advanced and tore it into tatters. The result was a spirited argument, in which Miss Gussie held her own with such ability that I was utterly routed and found another grievance against her. It was very humiliating to be worsted by a girl—a country girl at that, who had passed most of her life on a farm! No doubt she was strong-minded and wanted to vote. I was quite prepared to believe anything of her.

After tea Miss Ashley proposed a walk around the premises, in order to initiate me into my duties. Apart from his farm, Mr. Ashley owned large grist- and saw-mills and did a flourishing business, with the details of which Miss Gussie seemed so conversant that I lost all doubt of her ability to run the whole thing as she had claimed. I felt quite ignorant in the light of her superior knowledge, and our walk was enlivened by some rather too lively discussions between us. We walked about together, however, till the shadows of the firs by the mills stretched nearly across the pond and the white moon began to put on a silvery burnish. Then we wound up by a bitter dispute, during which Gussie's eyes were very black and each cheek had a round, red stain on it. She had a little air of triumph at having defeated me.

"I have to go now and see about putting away the milk, and I dare say you're not sorry to be rid of me," she said, with a demureness I had not credited her with, "but if you come to the verandah in half an hour I'll bring you out a glass of new milk and some pound cake I made today by a recipe that's been in the family for one hundred years, and I hope it will choke you for all the snubs you've been giving me." She walked away after this amiable wish, and I stood by the pond till the salmon tints faded from its waters and stars began to mirror themselves brokenly in its ripples. The mellow air was full of sweet, mingled eventide sounds as I walked back to the house. Aunt Lucy was knitting on the verandah. Gussie brought out cake and milk and chatted to us while we ate, in an inconsequent girlish way, or fed bits of cake to a green-eyed goblin in the likeness of a black cat.

She appeared in such an amiable light that I was half inclined to reconsider my opinion of her. When I went to my room the vase full of crimson leaves on my table suggested Gussie, and I repented of my unfriendliness for a moment —and only for a moment. Gussie and her mother passed through the hall below, and Aunt Lucy's soft voice floated up through my half-open door.

"Well, how do you like your cousin, my dear?"

Whereat that decided young lady promptly answered, "I think he is the most conceited youth I've met for some time."

Pleasant, wasn't it? I thought of Nellie's meek admiration of all my words and ways, and got her photo out to soothe my vanity. For the first time it struck me that her features were somewhat insipid. The thought seemed like disloyalty, so I banished it and went to bed.

I expected to dream of that disagreeable Gussie, but I did not, and I slept so soundly that it was ten o'clock the next morning before I woke. I sprang out of bed in dismay, dressed hastily, and ran down, not a little provoked at myself. Through the window I saw Gussie in the garden digging up some geraniums. She was enveloped in a clay-stained brown apron, a big flapping straw hat half hid her face, and she wore a pair of muddy old kid gloves. Her whole appearance was disreputable, and the face she turned to me as I said "Good morning" had a diagonal streak of clay across it. I added slovenliness to my already long list of her demerits.

"Good afternoon, rather. Don't you know what time it is? The men were here three hours ago for their orders. I thought it a pity to disturb your peaceful dreams, so I gave them myself and sent them off."

I was angrier than ever. A nice beginning I had made. And was that girl laughing at me?

"I expected to be called in time, certainly," I said stiffly. "I am not accustomed to oversleep myself. I promise it will not occur again."

My dignity was quite lost on Gussie. She peeled off her gloves cheerfully and said, "I suppose you'd like some breakfast. Just wait till I wash my hands and I'll get you some. Then if you're pining to be useful you can help me take up these geraniums."

There was no help for it. After I had breakfasted I went, with many misgivings. We got on fairly well, however. Gussie was particularly lively and kept me too busy for argument. I quite enjoyed the time and we did not quarrel until nearly the last, when we fell out bitterly over some horticultural problem and went in to dinner in sulky silence. Gussie disappeared after dinner and I saw no more of her. I was glad of this, but after a time I began to find it a little dull. Even a dispute would have been livelier. I visited the mills, looked over the farm, and then carelessly asked Aunt Lucy where Miss Ashley was. Aunt Lucy replied that she had gone to visit a friend and would not be back till the next day.

This was satisfactory, of course, highly so. What a relief it was to be rid of that girl with her self-assertiveness and independence. I said to myself that I hoped her friend would keep her for a week. I forgot to be disappointed that she had not when, next afternoon, I saw Gussie coming in at the gate with a tolerably large satchel and an armful of golden rod. I sauntered down to relieve her, and we had a sharp argument under way before we were halfway up the lane. As usual Gussie refused to give in that she was wrong.

Her walk had brought a faint, clear tint to her cheeks and her rippling dusky hair had half slipped down on her neck. She said she had to make some cookies for tea and if I had nothing better to do I might go and talk to her while she mixed them. It was not a gracious invitation but I went, rather than be left to my own company.

By the end of the week I was as much at home at Ashley Mills as if I had lived there all my life. Gussie and I were thrown together a good deal, for lack of other companions, and I saw no reason to change my opinion of her. She could be lively and entertaining when she chose, and at times she might be called beautiful. Still, I did not approve of her—at least I thought so, most of the time. Once in a while came a state of feeling which I did not quite understand.

One evening I went to prayer meeting with Aunt Lucy and Gussie. I had not seen the minister of Ashley Mills before, though Gussie and her mother seemed to know him intimately. I had an idea that he was old and silvery-haired and benevolent-looking. So I was rather surprised to find him as young as myself—a tall, pale, intellectual-looking man, with a high, white brow and dark, earnest eyes—decidedly attractive.

I was still more surprised when, after the service, he joined Gussie at the door and went down the steps with her. I felt distinctly ill-treated as I fell back with Aunt Lucy. There was no reason why I should—none; it ought to have been a relief. Rev. Carroll Martin had every right to see Miss Ashley home if he chose. Doubtless a girl who knew all there was to be known about business, farming, and milling, to say nothing of housekeeping and gardening, could discuss theology also. It was none of my business.

I don't know what kept me awake so late that night. As a consequence I overslept myself. I had managed to redeem my reputation on this point, but here it was lost again. I felt cross and foolish and cantankerous when I went out.

There was some unusual commotion at the well. It was an old-fashioned open one, with a chain and windlass. Aunt Lucy was peering anxiously down its mouth, from which a ladder was sticking. Just as I got there Gussie emerged from its depths with a triumphant face. Her skirt was muddy and draggled, her hair had tumbled down, and she held a dripping black cat.

"Coco must have fallen into the well last night," she explained, as I helped her to the ground. "I missed him at milking-time, and when I came to the well this morning I heard the most ear-splitting yowls coming up from it. I couldn't think where he could possibly be, for the water was quite calm, until I saw he had crept into a little crevice in the stones on the side. So I got a ladder and went down after him."

"You should have called me," I said sourly. "You might have killed yourself, going down there."

"And Coco might have tumbled in and drowned while you were getting up," retorted Gussie. "Besides, what was the need? I could go down as well as you."

"No doubt," I said, more sharply than I had any business to. "I don't dream of disputing your ability to do anything you may take it into your head to do. Most young ladies are not in the habit of going down wells, however."

"Perhaps not," she rejoined, with freezing calmness. "But, as you may have discovered, I am not 'most young ladies.' I am myself, Augusta Ashley, and accountable to nobody but myself if I choose to go down the well every day for pure love of it."

She walked off in her wet dress with her muddy cat. Gussie Ashley was the only girl I ever saw who could be dignified under such circumstances.

I was in a very bad humour with myself as I went off to see about having the well cleaned out. I had offended Gussie and I knew she would not be easily appeased. Nor was she. For a week she kept me politely, studiously, at a distance, in spite of my most humble advances. Rev. Carroll was a frequent caller, ostensibly to make arrangements about a Sunday school they were organizing in a poor part of the community. Gussie and he held long conversations on this enthralling subject. Then Gussie went on another visit to her friend, and when she came back so did Rev. Carroll.

One calm, hazy afternoon I was coming slowly up from the mills. Happening to glance at the kitchen roof, I gasped. It was on fire in one place. Evidently the dry shingles had caught fire from a spark. There was not a soul about save Gussie, Aunt Lucy, and myself. I dashed wildly into the kitchen, where Gussie was peeling apples.

"The house is on fire," I exclaimed. Gussie dropped her knife and turned pale.

"Don't wake Mother," was all she said, as she snatched a bucket of water from the table. The ladder was still lying by the well. In a second I had raised it to the roof and, while Gussie went up it like a squirrel and dashed the water on the flames, I had two more buckets ready for her.

Fortunately the fire had made little headway, though a few minutes more would have given it a dangerous start. The flames hissed and died out as Gussie threw on the water, and in a few seconds only a small black hole in the shingles remained. Gussie slid down the ladder. She trembled in every limb, but she put out her wet hand to me with a faint, triumphant smile. We shook hands across the ladder with a cordiality never before expressed.

For the next week, in spite of Rev. Carroll, I was happy when I thought of Gussie and miserable when I thought of Nellie. I held myself in some way bound to her and—was she not my ideal? Undoubtedly!

One day I got a letter from my sister. It was long and newsy, and the eighth page was most interesting.

"If you don't come home and look after Nellie," wrote Kate, "you'll soon not have her to look after. You remember that old lover of hers, Rod Allen? Well, he's home from the west now, immensely rich, they say, and his attentions to Nellie are the town talk. I think she likes him too. If you bury yourself any longer at Ashley Mills I won't be responsible for the consequences."

This lifted an immense weight from my mind, but the ninth page hurled it back again.

"You never say anything of Miss Ashley in your letters. What is she like—young or old, ugly or pretty, clever or dull? I met a lady recently who knows her and thinks she is charming. She also said Miss Ashley was to be married soon to Rev. Something-or-Other. Is it true?"

Aye, was it? Quite likely. Kate's letter made a very miserable man of me. Gussie found me a dull companion that day. After several vain attempts to rouse me to interest she gave it up.

"There's no use talking to you," she said impatiently. "I believe you are homesick. That letter you got this morning looked suspicious. Anyhow, I hope you'll get over it before I get back."

"Are you going away again?" I asked.

"Yes. I am going to stay a few days with Flossie." Flossie was that inseparable chum of hers.

"You seem to spend a good deal of your time with her," I remarked discontentedly.

Gussie opened her eyes at my tone.

"Why, of course," she said. "Flossie and I have always been chums. And she needs me more than ever just now, for she is awfully busy. She is to be married next month."

"Oh, I see—and you—"

"I'm to be bridesmaid, of course, and we've heaps to do. Flossie wanted to wait until Christmas, but Mr. Martin is in a—"

"Mr. Martin," I interrupted. "Is Mr. Martin going to marry your friend?"

"Why, yes. Didn't you know? They just suit each other. There he comes now. He's going to drive me over, and I'm not ready. Talk to him, for pity's sake, while I go and dress."

I never enjoyed a conversation more. Rev. Carroll Martin was a remarkably interesting man.

Nellie married Rod Allen at Christmas and I was best man. Nellie made a charming little bride, and Rod fairly worshipped her. My own wedding did not come off until spring, as Gussie said she could not get ready before that.

Kismet

The fifth heat in the free-for-all was just over. "Lu-Lu" had won, and the crowd on the grand stand and the hangers-on around the track were cheering themselves hoarse. Clear through the noisy clamour shrilled a woman's cry.

"Ah—I have dropped my scorecard."

A man in front of her turned.

"I have an extra one, madame. Will you accept it?"

Her small, modishly-gloved hand closed eagerly on it before she lifted her eyes to his face. Both started convulsively. The man turned very pale, but the woman's ripe-tinted face coloured darkly.

"You?" she faltered.

His lips parted in the coldly-grave smile she remembered and hated.

"You are not glad to see me," he said calmly, "but that, I suppose, was not to be expected. I did not come here to annoy you. This meeting is as unexpected to me as to you. I had no suspicion that for the last half-hour I had been standing next to my—"

She interrupted him by an imperious gesture. Still clutching the scorecard she half-turned from him. Again he smiled, this time with a tinge of scorn, and shifted his eyes to the track.

None of the people around them had noticed the little by-play. All eyes were on the track, which was being cleared for the first heat of another race. The free-for-all horses were being led away blanketed. The crowd cheered "Lu-Lu" as she went past, a shapeless oddity. The backers of "Mascot", the rival favourite, looked gloomy.

The woman noticed nothing of all this. She was small, very pretty, still young, and gowned in a quite unmistakable way. She studied the man's profile furtively. He looked older than when she had seen him last—there were some silver threads gleaming in his close-clipped dark hair and short, pointed beard. Otherwise there was little change in the quiet features and somewhat stern grey eyes. She wondered if he had cared at all.

They had not met for five years. She shut her eyes and looked in on her past. It all came back very vividly. She had been eighteen when they were married—a gay, high-spirited girl and the season's beauty. He was much older and a quiet, serious student. Her friends had wondered why she married him—sometimes she wondered herself, but she had loved him, or thought so.

The marriage had been an unhappy one. She was fond of society and gaiety, he wanted quiet and seclusion. She Was impulsive and impatient, he deliberate and grave. The strong wills clashed. After two years of an unbearable sort of life they had separated—quietly, and without scandal of any sort. She had wanted a divorce, but he would not agree to that, so she had taken her own independent fortune and gone back to her own way of life. In the following five years she had succeeded in burying all remembrance well out of sight. No one knew if she were satisfied or not; her world was charitable to her and she lived a gay and quite irreproachable life. She wished that she had not come to the races. It was such an irritating encounter. She opened her eyes wearily; the dusty track, the flying horses, the gay dresses of the women on the grandstand, the cloudless blue sky, the brilliant September sunshine, the purple distances all commingled in a glare that made her head ache. Before it all she saw the tall figure by her side, his face turned from her, watching the track intently.

She wondered with a vague curiosity what induced him to come to the races. Such things were not greatly in his line. Evidently their chance meeting had not disturbed him. It was a sign that he did not care. She sighed a little wearily and closed her eyes. When the heat was over he turned to her.

"May I ask how you have been since—since we met last? You are looking extremely well. Has Vanity Fair palled in any degree?"

She was angry at herself and him. Where had her careless society manner and well-bred composure gone? She felt weak and hysterical. What if she should burst into tears before the whole crowd—before those coldly critical grey eyes? She almost hated him.

"No—why should it? I have found it very pleasant—and I have been well —very well. And you?"

He jotted down the score carefully before he replied.

"I? Oh, a book-worm and recluse always leads a placid life. I never cared for excitement, you know. I came down here to attend a sale of some rare editions, and a well-meaning friend dragged me out to see the races. I find it rather interesting, I must confess, much more so than I should have fancied. Sorry I can't stay until the end. I must go as soon as the free-for-all is over, if not before. I have backed 'Mascot'; you?"

"'Lu-Lu'" she answered quickly—it almost seemed defiantly. How horribly unreal it was—this carrying on of small talk, as if they were the merest of chance-met acquaintances! "She belongs to a friend of mine, so I am naturally interested."

"She and 'Mascot' are ties now—both have won two heats. One more for either will decide it. This is a good day for the races. Excuse me."

He leaned over and brushed a scrap of paper from her grey cloak. She shivered slightly.

"You are cold! This stand is draughty."

"I am not at all cold, thank you. What race is this?—oh! the three-minute one."

She bent forward with assumed interest to watch the scoring. She was breathing heavily. There were tears in her eyes—she bit her lips savagely and glared at the track until they were gone.

Presently he spoke again, in the low, even tone demanded by circumstances.

"This is a curious meeting, is it not?—quite a flavor of romance! By-the-way, do you read as many novels as ever?"

She fancied there was mockery in his tone. She remembered how very frivolous he used to consider her novel-reading. Besides, she resented the personal tinge. What right had he?

"Almost as many," she answered carelessly.

"I was very intolerant, wasn't I?" he said after a pause. "You thought so—you were right. You have been happier since you—left me?"

"Yes," she said defiantly, looking straight into his eyes.

"And you do not regret it?"

He bent down a little. His sleeve brushed against her shoulder. Something in his face arrested the answer she meant to make.

"I—I—did not say that," she murmured faintly.

There was a burst of cheering. The free-for-all horses were being brought out for the sixth heat. She turned away to watch them. The scoring began, and seemed likely to have no end. She was tired of it all. It didn't matter a pin to her whether "Lu-Lu" or "Mascot" won. What did matter! Had Vanity Fair after all been a satisfying exchange for love? He had loved her once, and they had been happy at first. She had never before said, even in her own heart: "I am sorry," but—suddenly, she felt his hand on her shoulder, and looked up. Their eyes met. He stooped and said almost in a whisper:

"Will you come back to me?"

"I don't know," she whispered breathlessly, as one half-fascinated.

"We were both to blame—but I the most. I was too hard on you—I ought to have made more allowance. We are wiser now both of us. Come back to me —my wife."

His tone was cold and his face expressionless. It was on her lips to cry out "No," passionately.

But the slender, scholarly hand on her shoulder was trembling with the intensity of his repressed emotion. He did care, then. A wild caprice flashed into her brain. She sprang up.

"See," she cried, "they're off now. This heat will probably decide the race. If 'Lu-Lu' wins I will not go back to you, if 'Mascot' does I will. That is my decision."

He turned paler, but bowed in assent. He knew by bitter experience how unchangeable her whims were, how obstinately she clung to even the most absurd.

She leaned forward breathlessly. The crowd hung silently on the track. "Lu-Lu" and "Mascot" were neck and neck, getting in splendid work. Half-way round the course "Lu-Lu" forged half a neck ahead, and her backers went mad. But one woman dropped her head in her hands and dared look no more. One man with white face and set lips watched the track unswervingly.

Again "Mascot" crawled up, inch by inch. They were on the home stretch, they were equal, the cheering broke out, then silence, then another terrific burst, shouts, yells and clappings—"Mascot" had won the free-for-all. In the front row a woman stood up, swayed and shaken as a leaf in the wind. She straightened her scarlet hat and readjusted her veil unsteadily. There was a smile on her lips and tears in her eyes. No one noticed her. A man beside her drew her hand through his arm in a quiet proprietary fashion. They left the grand stand together.

Lilian's Business Venture

Lilian Mitchell turned into the dry-goods store on Randall Street, just as Esther Miller and Ella Taylor came out. They responded coldly to her greeting and exchanged significant glances as they walked away.

Lilian's pale face crimsoned. She was a tall, slender girl of about seventeen, and dressed in mourning. These girls had been her close friends once. But that was before the Mitchells had lost their money. Since then Lilian had been cut by many of her old chums and she felt it keenly.

The clerks in the store were busy and Lilian sat down to wait her turn. Near to her two ladies were also waiting and chatting.

"Helen wants me to let her have a birthday party," Mrs. Saunders was saying wearily. "She has been promised it so long and I hate to disappoint the child, but our girl left last week, and I cannot possibly make all the cakes and things myself. I haven't the time or strength, so Helen must do without her party."

"Talking of girls," said Mrs. Reeves impatiently, "I am almost discouraged.

It is so hard to get a good all-round one. The last one I had was so saucy I had to discharge her, and the one I have now cannot make decent bread. I never had good luck with bread myself either."

"That is Mrs. Porter's great grievance too. It is no light task to bake bread for all those boarders. Have you made your jelly yet?"

"No. Maria cannot make it, she says, and I detest messing with jelly. But I really must see to it soon."

At this point a saleswoman came up to Lilian, who made her small purchases and went out.

"There goes Lilian Mitchell," said Mrs. Reeves in an undertone. "She looks very pale. They say they are dreadfully poor since Henry Mitchell died. His affairs were in a bad condition, I am told."

"I am sorry for Mrs. Mitchell," responded Mrs. Saunders. "She is such a sweet woman. Lilian will have to do something, I suppose, and there is so little chance for a girl here."

Lilian, walking down the street, was wearily turning over in her mind the problems of her young existence. Her father had died the preceding spring. He had been a supposedly prosperous merchant; the Mitchells had always lived well, and Lilian was a petted and only child. Then came the shock of Henry Mitchell's sudden death and of financial ruin. His affairs were found to be hopelessly involved; when all the debts were paid there was left only the merest pittance—barely enough for house-rent—for Lilian and her mother to live upon. They had moved into a tiny cottage in an unfashionable locality, and during the summer Lilian had tried hard to think of something to do. Mrs. Mitchell was a delicate woman, and the burden of their situation fell on Lilian's young shoulders.

There seemed to be no place for her. She could not teach and had no particular talent in any line. There was no opening for her in Willington, which was a rather sleepy little place, and Lilian was almost in despair.

"There really doesn't seem to be any real place in the world for me, Mother," she said rather dolefully at the supper table. "I've no talent at all; it is dreadful to have been born without one. And yet I must do something, and do it soon."

And Lilian, after she had washed up the tea dishes, went upstairs and had a good cry.

But the darkest hour, so the proverb goes, is just before the dawn, and after Lilian had had her cry out and was sitting at her window in the dusk, watching a thin new moon shining over the trees down the street, her inspiration came to her. A minute later she whirled into the tiny sitting-room where her mother was sewing.

"Mother, our fortune is made! I have an idea!"

"Don't lose it, then," said Mrs. Mitchell with a smile. "What is it, my dear?"

Lilian sobered herself, sat down by her mother's side, and proceeded to recount the conversation she had heard in the store that afternoon.

"Now, Mother, this is where my brilliant idea comes in. You have often told me I am a born cook and I always have good luck. Now, tomorrow morning I shall go to Mrs. Saunders and offer to furnish all the good things for Helen's birthday party, and then I'll ask Mrs. Reeves and Mrs. Porter if I may make their bread for them. That will do for a beginning, I like cooking, you know, and I believe that in time I can work up a good business."

"It seems to be a good idea," said Mrs. Mitchell thoughtfully, "and I am willing that you should try. But have you thought it all out carefully? There will be many difficulties."

"I know. I don't expect smooth sailing right along, and perhaps I'll fail altogether; but somehow I don't believe I will."

"A great many of your old friends will think—"

"Oh, yes; I know that too, but I am not going to mind it, Mother. I don't think there is any disgrace in working for my living. I'm going to do my best and not care what people say."

Early next morning Lilian started out. She had carefully thought over the details of her small venture, considered ways and means, and decided on the most advisable course. She would not attempt too much, and she felt sure of success.

To secure competent servants was one of the problems of Willington people. At Drayton, a large neighbouring town, were several factories, and into these all the working girls from Willington had crowded, leaving very few who were willing to go out to service. Many of those who did were poor cooks, and Lilian shrewdly suspected that many a harassed housekeeper in the village would be glad to avail herself of the new enterprise.

Lilian was, as she had said of herself, "a born cook." This was her capital, and she meant to make the most of it. Mrs. Saunders listened to her businesslike details with surprise and delight.

"It is the very thing," she said. "Helen is so eager for that party, but I could not undertake it myself. Her birthday is Friday. Can you have everything ready by then?"

"Yes, I think so," said Lilian briskly, producing her notebook. "Please give me the list of what you want and I will do my best."

From Mrs. Saunders she went to Mrs. Reeves and found a customer as soon as she had told the reason of her call. "I'll furnish all the bread and rolls you need," she said, "and they will be good, too. Now, about your jelly. I can make good jelly, and I'll be very glad to make yours."

When she left, Lilian had an order for two dozen glasses of apple jelly, as well as a standing one for bread and rolls. Mrs. Porter was next visited and grasped eagerly at the opportunity.

"I know your bread will be good," she said, "and you may count on me as a regular customer."

Lilian thought she had enough on hand for a first attempt and went home satisfied. On her way she called at the grocery store with an order that surprised Mr. Hooper. When she told him of her plan he opened his eyes.

"I must tell my wife about that. She isn't strong and she doesn't like cooking."

After dinner Lilian went to work, enveloped in a big apron, and whipped eggs, stoned raisins, stirred, concocted, and baked until dark. When bedtime came she was so tired that she could hardly crawl upstairs; but she felt happy too, for the day had been a successful one.

And so also were the days and weeks and months that followed. It was hard and constant work, but it brought its reward. Lilian had not promised more than she could perform, and her customers were satisfied. In a short time she found herself with a regular and growing business on her hands, for new customers were gradually added and always came to stay.

People who gave parties found it very convenient to follow Mrs. Saunders's example and order their supplies from Lilian. She had a very busy winter and, of course, it was not all plain sailing. She had many difficulties to contend with. Sometimes days came on which everything seemed to go wrong—when the stove smoked or the oven wouldn't heat properly, when cakes fell flat and bread was sour and pies behaved as only totally depraved pies can, when she burned her fingers and felt like giving up in despair.

Then, again, she found herself cut by several of her old acquaintances. But she was too sensible to worry much over this. The friends really worth having were still hers, her mother's face had lost its look of care, and her business was prospering. She was hopeful and wide awake, kept her wits about her and looked out for hints, and learned to laugh over her failures.

During the winter she and her mother had managed to do most of the work themselves, hiring little Mary Robinson next door on especially busy days, and now and then calling in the assistance of Jimmy Bowen and his hand sled to carry orders to customers. But when spring came Lilian prepared to open up her summer campaign on a much larger scale. Mary Robinson was hired for the season, and John Perkins was engaged to act as carrier with his express wagon. A summer kitchen was boarded in in the backyard, and a new range bought; Lilian began operations with a striking advertisement in the Willington News and an attractive circular sent around to all her patrons. Picnics and summer weddings were frequent. In bread and rolls her trade was brisk and constant. She also took orders for pickles, preserves, and jellies, and this became such a flourishing branch that a second assistant had to be hired.

It was a cardinal rule with Lilian never to send out any article that was not up to her standard. She bore the loss of her failures, and sometimes stayed up half of the night to fill an order on time. "Prompt and perfect" was her motto.

The long hot summer days were very trying, and sometimes she got very tired of it all. But when on the anniversary of her first venture she made up her accounts she was well pleased. To be sure, she had not made a fortune; but she had paid all their expenses, had a hundred dollars clear, and had laid the solid foundations of a profitable business.

"Mother," she said jubilantly, as she wiped a dab of flour from her nose and proceeded to concoct the icing for Blanche Remington's wedding cake, "don't you think my business venture has been a decided success?"

Mrs. Mitchell surveyed her busy daughter with a motherly smile. "Yes, I think it has," she said.

Miriam's Lover

I had been reading a ghost story to Mrs. Sefton, and I laid it down at the end with a little shrug of contempt.

"What utter nonsense!" I said.

Mrs. Sefton nodded abstractedly above her fancywork.

"That is. It is a very commonplace story indeed. I don't believe the spirits of the departed trouble themselves to revisit the glimpses of the moon for the purpose of frightening honest mortals—or even for the sake of hanging around the favourite haunts of their existence in the flesh. If they ever appear, it must be for a better reason than that."

"You don't surely think that they ever do appear?" I said incredulously.

"We have no proof that they do not, my dear."

"Surely, Mary," I exclaimed, "you don't mean to say that you believe people ever do or can see spirits—ghosts, as the word goes?"

"I didn't say I believed it. I never saw anything of the sort. I neither believe nor disbelieve. But you know queer things do happen at times—things you can't account for. At least, people who you know wouldn't lie say so. Of course, they may be mistaken. And I don't think that everybody can see spirits either, provided they are to be seen. It requires people of a certain organization—with a spiritual eye, as it were. We haven't all got that—in fact, I think very few of us have. I dare say you think I'm talking nonsense."

"Well, yes, I think you are. You really surprise me, Mary. I always thought you the least likely person in the world to take up with such ideas. Something must have come under your observation to develop such theories in your practical head. Tell me what it was."

"To what purpose? You would remain as sceptical as ever."

"Possibly not. Try me; I may be convinced."

"No," returned Mrs. Sefton calmly. "Nobody ever is convinced by hearsay. When a person has once seen a spirit—or thinks he has—he thenceforth believes it. And when somebody else is intimately associated with that person and knows all the circumstances—well, he admits the possibility, at least. That is my position. But by the time it gets to the third person—the outsider—it loses power. Besides, in this particular instance the story isn't very exciting. But then—it's true."

"You have excited my curiosity. You must tell me the story."

"Well, first tell me what you think of this. Suppose two people, both sensitively organized individuals, loved each other with a love stronger than life. If they were apart, do you think it might be possible for their souls to communicate with each other in some inexplicable way? And if anything happened to one, don't you think that that one could and would let the spirit of the other know?"

"You're getting into too deep waters for me, Mary," I said, shaking my head. "I'm not an authority on telepathy, or whatever you call it. But I've no belief in such theories. In fact, I think they are all nonsense. I'm sure you must think so too in your rational moments."

"I dare say it is all nonsense," said Mrs. Sefton slowly, "but if you had lived a whole year in the same house with Miriam Gordon, you would have been tainted too. Not that she had 'theories'—at least, she never aired them if she had. But there was simply something about the girl herself that gave a person strange impressions. When I first met her I had the most uncanny feeling that she was all spirit—soul—what you will! no flesh, anyhow. That feeling wore off after a while, but she never seemed like other people to me.

"She was Mr. Sefton's niece. Her father had died when she was a child. When Miriam was twenty her mother had married a second time and went to Europe with her husband. Miriam came to live with us while they were away. Upon their return she was herself to be married.

"I had never seen Miriam before. Her arrival was unexpected, and I was absent from home when she came. I returned in the evening, and when I saw her first she was standing under the chandelier in the drawing room. Talk about spirits! For five seconds I thought I had seen one.

"Miriam was a beauty. I had known that before, though I think I hardly expected to see such wonderful loveliness. She was tall and extremely graceful, dark—at least her hair was dark, but her skin was wonderfully fair and clear. Her hair was gathered away from her face, and she had a high, pure, white forehead, and the straightest, finest, blackest brows. Her face was oval, with very large and dark eyes.

"I soon realized that Miriam was in some mysterious fashion different from other people. I think everyone who met her felt the same way. Yet it was a feeling hard to define. For my own part I simply felt as if she belonged to another world, and that part of the time she—her soul, you know—was back there again.

"You must not suppose that Miriam was a disagreeable person to have in the house. On the contrary, it was the very reverse. Everybody liked her. She was one of the sweetest, most winsome girls I ever knew, and I soon grew to love her dearly. As for what Dick called her 'little queernesses'—well, we got used to them in time.

"Miriam was engaged, as I have told you, to a young Harvard man named Sidney Claxton. I knew she loved him very deeply. When she showed me his photograph, I liked his appearance and said so. Then I made some teasing remark about her love-letters—just for a joke, you know. Miriam looked at me with an odd little smile and said quickly:

"'Sidney and I never write to each other.'

"'Why, Miriam!' I exclaimed in astonishment. 'Do you mean to tell me you never hear from him at all?'

"'No, I did not say that. I hear from him every day—every hour. We do not need to write letters. There are better means of communication between two souls that are in perfect accord with each other.'

"'Miriam, you uncanny creature, what do you mean?' I asked.

"But Miriam only gave another queer smile and made no answer at all. Whatever her beliefs or theories were, she would never discuss them.

"She had a habit of dropping into abstracted reveries at any time or place. No matter where she was, this, whatever it was, would come over her. She would sit there, perhaps in the centre of a gay crowd, and gaze right out into space, not hearing or seeing a single thing that went on around her.

"I remember one day in particular; we were sewing in my room. I looked up and saw that Miriam's work had dropped on her knee and she was leaning forward, her lips apart, her eyes gazing upward with an unearthly expression.

"'Don't look like that, Miriam!' I said, with a little shiver. 'You seem to be looking at something a thousand miles away!'

"Miriam came out of her trance or reverie and said, with a little laugh:

"'How do you know but that I was?'

"She bent her head for a minute or two. Then she lifted it again and looked at me with a sudden contraction of her level brows that betokened vexation.

"'I wish you hadn't spoken to me just then,' she said. 'You interrupted the message I was receiving. I shall not get it at all now.'

"'Miriam,' I implored. 'I so wish my dear girl, that you wouldn't talk so. It makes people think there is something queer about you. Who in the world was sending you a message, as you call it?'

"'Sidney,' said Miriam simply.

"'Nonsense!'

"'You think it is nonsense because you don't understand it,' was her calm response.

"I recall another event was when some caller dropped in and we had drifted into a discussion about ghosts and the like—and I've no doubt we all talked some delicious nonsense. Miriam said nothing at the time, but when we were alone I asked her what she thought of it.

"'I thought you were all merely talking against time,' she retorted evasively.

"'But, Miriam, do you really think it is possible for ghosts—'

"'I detest that word!'

"'Well, spirits then—to return after death, or to appear to anyone apart from the flesh?'

"'I will tell you what I know. If anything were to happen to Sidney—if he were to die or be killed—he would come to me himself and tell me.'

"One day Miriam came down to lunch looking pale and worried. After Dick went out, I asked her if anything were wrong.

"'Something has happened to Sidney,' she replied, 'some painful accident—I don't know what.'

"'How do you know?' I cried. Then, as she looked at me strangely, I added hastily, 'You haven't been receiving any more unearthly messages, have you? Surely, Miriam, you are not so foolish as to really believe in that!'

"'I know,' she answered quickly. 'Belief or disbelief has nothing to do with it. Yes, I have had a message. I know that some accident has happened to Sidney—painful and inconvenient but not particularly dangerous. I do not know what it is. Sidney will write me that. He writes when it is absolutely necessary.'

"'Aerial communication isn't perfected yet then?' I said mischievously. But, observing how really worried she seemed, I added, 'Don't fret, Miriam. You may be mistaken.'

"Well, two days afterwards she got a note from her lover—the first I had ever known her to receive—in which he said he had been thrown from his horse and had broken his left arm. It had happened the very morning Miriam received her message.

"Miriam had been with us about eight months when one day she came into my room hurriedly. She was very pale.

"'Sidney is ill—dangerously ill. What shall I do?'

"I knew she must have had another of those abominable messages—or thought she had—and really, remembering the incident of the broken arm, I couldn't feel as sceptical as I pretended to. I tried to cheer her, but did not succeed. Two hours later she had a telegram from her lover's college chum, saying that Mr. Claxton was dangerously ill with typhoid fever.

"I was quite alarmed about Miriam in the days that followed. She grieved and fretted continually. One of her troubles was that she received no more messages; she said it was because Sidney was too ill to send them. Anyhow, she had to content herself with the means of communication used by ordinary mortals.

"Sidney's mother, who had gone to nurse him, wrote every day, and at last good news came. The crisis was over and the doctor in attendance thought

Sidney would recover. Miriam seemed like a new creature then, and rapidly recovered her spirits.

"For a week reports continued favourable. One night we went to the opera to hear a celebrated prima donna. When we returned home Miriam and I were sitting in her room, chatting over the events of the evening.

"Suddenly she sat straight up with a sort of convulsive shudder, and at the same time—you may laugh if you like—the most horrible feeling came over me. I didn't see anything, but I just felt that there was something or someone in the room besides ourselves.

"Miriam was gazing straight before her. She rose to her feet and held out her hands.

"'Sidney!' she said.

"Then she fell to the floor in a dead faint.

"I screamed for Dick, rang the bell and rushed to her.

"In a few minutes the whole household was aroused, and Dick was off posthaste for the doctor, for we could not revive Miriam from her death-like swoon. She seemed as one dead. We worked over her for hours. She would come out of her faint for a moment, give us an unknowing stare and go shudderingly off again.

"The doctor talked of some fearful shock, but I kept my own counsel. At dawn Miriam came back to life at last. When she and I were left alone, she turned to me.

"'Sidney is dead,' she said quietly. 'I saw him—just before I fainted. I looked up, and he was standing between me and you. He had come to say farewell.'

"What could I say? Almost while we were talking a telegram came. He was dead—he had died at the very hour at which Miriam had seen him."

Mrs. Sefton paused, and the lunch bell rang.

"What do you think of it?" she queried as we rose.

"Honestly, I don't know what I think of it," I answered frankly.

Miss Calista's Peppermint Bottle

Miss Calista was perplexed. Her nephew, Caleb Cramp, who had been her right-hand man for years and whom she had got well broken into her ways, had gone to the Klondike, leaving her to fill his place with the next best man; but the next best man was slow to appear, and meanwhile Miss Calista was looking about her warily. She could afford to wait a while, for the crop was all in and the fall ploughing done, so that the need of a successor to Caleb was not as pressing as it might otherwise have been. There was no lack of applicants, such as they were. Miss Calista was known to be a kind and generous mistress, although she had her "ways," and insisted calmly and immovably upon wholehearted compliance with them. She had a small, well-cultivated farm and a comfortable house, and her hired men lived in clover. Caleb Cramp had been perfection after his kind, and Miss Calista did not expect to find his equal. Nevertheless, she set up a certain standard of requirements; and although three weeks, during which Miss Calista had been obliged to put up with the immature services of a neighbour's boy, had elapsed since Caleb's departure, no one had as yet stepped into his vacant and coveted shoes.

Certainly Miss Calista was somewhat hard to please, but she was not thinking of herself as she sat by her front window in the chilly November twilight. Instead, she was musing on the degeneration of hired men, and reflecting that it was high time the wheat was thrashed, the house banked, and sundry other duties attended to.

Ches Maybin had been up that afternoon to negotiate for the vacant place, and had offered to give satisfaction for smaller wages than Miss Calista had ever paid. But he had met with a brusque refusal, scarcely as civil as Miss Calista had bestowed on drunken Jake Stinson from the Morrisvale Road.

Not that Miss Calista had any particular prejudice against Ches Maybin, or knew anything positively to his discredit. She was simply unconsciously following the example of a world that exerts itself to keep a man down when he is down and prevent all chance of his rising. Nothing succeeds like success, and the converse of this is likewise true—that nothing fails like failure. There was not a person in Cooperstown who would not have heartily endorsed Miss Calista's refusal.

Ches Maybin was only eighteen, although he looked several years older, and although no flagrant misdoing had ever been proved against him, suspicion of such was not wanting. He came of a bad stock, people said sagely, adding that what was bred in the bone was bound to come out in the flesh. His father, old Sam Maybin, had been a shiftless and tricky rascal, as everybody knew, and had ended his days in the poorhouse. Ches's mother had died when he was a baby, and he had come up somehow, in a hand-to-mouth fashion, with all the cloud of heredity hanging over him. He was always looked at askance, and when any mischief came to light in the village, it was generally fastened on him as a convenient and handy scapegoat. He was considered sulky and lazy, and the local prophets united in predicting a bad end for him sooner or later; and, moreover, diligently endeavoured by their general treatment of him to put him in a fair way to fulfil their predictions. Miss Calista, when she had shut Chester Maybin out into the chill gloom of the November dusk, dismissed him from her thoughts. There were other things of more moment to her just then than old Sam Maybin's hopeful son.

There was nobody in the house but herself, and although this was neither alarming nor unusual, it was unusual—and Miss Calista considered it alarming —that the sum of five hundred dollars should at that very moment be in the upper right-hand drawer of the sideboard, which sum had been up to the previous day safe in the coffers of the Millageville bank. But certain unfavourable rumours were in course of circulation about that same institution, and Miss Calista, who was nothing if not prudent, had gone to the bank that very morning and withdrawn her deposit. She intended to go over to Kerrytown the very next day and deposit it in the Savings Bank there. Not another day would she keep it in the house, and, indeed, it worried her to think she must keep it even for the night, as she had told Mrs. Galloway that afternoon during a neighbourly back-yard chat.

"Not but what it's safe enough," she said, "for not a soul but you knows I've got it. But I'm not used to have so much by me, and there are always tramps going round. It worries me somehow. I wouldn't give it a thought if Caleb was here. I s'pose being all alone makes me nervous."

Miss Calista was still rather nervous when she went to bed that night, but she was a woman of sound sense and was determined not to give way to foolish fears. She locked doors and windows carefully, as was her habit, and saw that the fastenings were good and secure. The one on the dining-room window, looking out on the back yard, wasn't; in fact, it was broken altogether; but, as Miss Calista told herself, it had been broken just so for the last six years, and nobody had ever tried to get in at it yet, and it wasn't likely anyone would begin tonight.

Miss Calista went to bed and, despite her worry, slept soon and soundly. It was well on past midnight when she suddenly wakened and sat bolt upright in bed. She was not accustomed to waken in the night, and she had the impression of having been awakened by some noise. She listened breathlessly. Her room was directly over the dining-room, and an empty stovepipe hole opened up through the ceiling of the latter at the head of her bed.

There was no mistake about it. Something or some person was moving about stealthily in the room below. It wasn't the cat—Miss Calista had shut him in the woodshed before she went to bed, and he couldn't possibly get out. It must certainly be a beggar or tramp of some description.

Miss Calista might be given over to nervousness in regard to imaginary thieves, but in the presence of real danger she was cool and self-reliant. As noiselessly and swiftly as any burglar himself, Miss Calista slipped out of bed and into her clothes. Then she tip-toed out into the hall. The late moonlight, streaming in through the hall windows, was quite enough illumination for her purpose, and she got downstairs and was fairly in the open doorway of the dining-room before a sound betrayed her presence.

Standing at the sideboard, hastily ransacking the neat contents of an open drawer, stood a man's figure, dimly visible in the moonlight gloom. As Miss Calista's grim form appeared in the doorway, the midnight marauder turned with a start and then, with an inarticulate cry, sprang, not at the courageous lady, but at the open window behind him.

Miss Calista, realizing with a flash of comprehension that he was escaping her, had a woman-like impulse to get a blow in anyhow; she grasped and hurled at her unceremonious caller the first thing that came to hand—a bottle of peppermint essence that was standing on the sideboard.

The missile hit the escaping thief squarely on the shoulder as he sprang out of the window, and the fragments of glass came clattering down on the sill. The next moment Miss Calista found herself alone, standing by the sideboard in a half-dazed fashion, for the whole thing had passed with such lightning-like rapidity that it almost seemed as if it were the dissolving end of a bad dream. But the open drawer and the window, where the bits of glass were glistening in the moonlight, were no dream. Miss Calista recovered herself speedily, closed the window, lit the lamp, gathered up the broken glass, and set up the chairs which the would-be thief had upset in his exit. An examination of the sideboard showed the precious five hundred safe and sound in an undisturbed drawer.

Miss Calista kept grim watch and ward there until morning, and thought the matter over exhaustively. In the end she resolved to keep her own counsel. She had no clue whatever to the thief's whereabouts or identity, and no good would come of making a fuss, which might only end in throwing suspicion on someone who might be quite innocent.

When the morning came Miss Calista lost no time in setting out for Kerrytown, where the money was soon safely deposited in the bank. She heaved a sigh of relief when she left the building.

I feel as if I could enjoy life once more, she said to herself. Goodness me, if I'd had to keep that money by me for a week itself, I'd have been a raving lunatic by the end of it.

Miss Calista had shopping to do and friends to visit in town, so that the dull autumn day was well nigh spent when she finally got back to Cooperstown and paused at the corner store to get a bundle of matches.

The store was full of men, smoking and chatting around the fire, and Miss Calista, whose pet abomination was tobacco smoke, was not at all minded to wait any longer than she could help. But Abiram Fell was attending to a previous customer, and Miss Calista sat grimly down by the counter to wait her turn.

The door opened, letting in a swirl of raw November evening wind and Ches Maybin. He nodded sullenly to Mr. Fell and passed down the store to mutter a message to a man at the further end.

Miss Calista lifted her head as he passed and sniffed the air as a charger who scents battle. The smell of tobacco was strong, and so was that of the open boxes of dried herring on the counter, but plainly, above all the commingled odours of a country grocery, Miss Calista caught a whiff of peppermint, so strong as to leave no doubt of its origin. There had been no hint of it before Ches Maybin's entrance.

The latter did not wait long. He was out and striding along the shadowy road when Miss Calista left the store and drove smartly after him. It never took Miss Calista long to make up her mind about anything, and she had weighed and passed judgement on Ches Maybin's case while Mr. Fell was doing up her matches.

The lad glanced up furtively as she checked her fat grey pony beside him.

"Good evening, Chester," she said with brisk kindness. "I can give you a lift, if you are going my way. Jump in, quick—Dapple is a little restless."

A wave of crimson, duskily perceptible under his sunburned skin, surged over Ches Maybin's face. It almost seemed as if he were going to blurt out a blunt refusal. But Miss Calista's face was so guileless and her tone so friendly, that he thought better of it and sprang in beside her, and Dapple broke into an impatient trot down the long hill lined with its bare, wind-writhen maples.

After a few minutes' silence Miss Calista turned to her moody companion.

"Chester," she said, as tranquilly as if about to ask him the most ordinary question in the world, "why did you climb into my house last night and try to steal my money?"

Ches Maybin started convulsively, as if he meant to spring from the buggy at once, but Miss Calista's hand was on his arm in a grasp none the less firm because of its gentleness, and there was a warning gleam in her grey eyes.

"It won't mend matters trying to get clear of me, Chester. I know it was you and I want an answer—a truthful one, mind you—to my question. I am your friend, and I am not going to harm you if you tell me the truth."

Her clear and incisive gaze met and held irresistibly the boy's wavering one. The sullen obstinacy of his face relaxed.

"Well," he muttered finally, "I was just desperate, that's why. I've never done anything real bad in my life before, but people have always been down on me. I'm blamed for everything, and nobody wants anything to do with me. I'm willing to work, but I can't get a thing to do. I'm in rags and I haven't a cent, and winter's coming on. I heard you telling Mrs. Galloway yesterday about the money. I was behind the fir hedge and you didn't see me. I went away and planned it all out. I'd get in some way—and I meant to use the money to get away out west as far from here as I could, and begin life there, where nobody knew me, and where I'd have some sort of a chance. I've never had any here. You can put me in jail now, if you like—they'll feed and clothe me there, anyhow, and I'll be on a level with the rest."

The boy had blurted it all out sullenly and half-chokingly. A world of rebellion and protest against the fate that had always dragged him down was couched in his voice.

Miss Calista drew Dapple to a standstill before her gate.

"I'm not going to send you to jail, Chester. I believe you've told me the truth. Yesterday you wanted me to give you Caleb's place and I refused. Well, I offer it to you now. If you'll come, I'll hire you, and give you as good wages as I gave him."

Ches Maybin looked incredulous.

"Miss Calista, you can't mean it."

"I do mean it, every word. You say you have never had a chance. Well, I am going to give you one—a chance to get on the right road and make a man of yourself. Nobody shall ever know about last night's doings from me, and I'll make it my business to forget them if you deserve it. What do you say?"

Ches lifted his head and looked her squarely in the face.

"I'll come," he said huskily. "It ain't no use to try and thank you, Miss Calista. But I'll live my thanks."

And he did. The good people of Cooperstown held up their hands in horror when they heard that Miss Calista had hired Ches Maybin, and prophesied that the deluded woman would live to repent her rash step. But not all prophecies come true. Miss Calista smiled serenely and kept on her own misguided way. And Ches Maybin proved so efficient and steady that the arrangement was continued, and in due time people outlived their old suspicions and came to regard him as a thoroughly smart and trustworthy young man.

"Miss Calista has made a man of Ches Maybin," said the oracles. "He ought to be very grateful to her."

And he was. But only he and Miss Calista and the peppermint bottle ever knew the precise extent of his gratitude, and they never told.

The Jest That Failed

"I think it is simply a disgrace to have a person like that in our class," said Edna Hayden in an injured tone.

"And she doesn't seem a bit ashamed of it, either," said Agnes Walters.

"Rather proud of it, I should say," returned her roommate, spitefully. "It seems to me that if I were so poor that I had to 'room' myself and dress as dowdily as she does that I really couldn't look anybody in the face. What must the boys think of her? And if it wasn't for her being in it, our class would be the smartest and dressiest in the college—even those top-lofty senior girls admit that."

"It's a shame," said Agnes, conclusively. "But she needn't expect to associate with our set. I, for one, won't have anything to do with her."

"Nor I. I think it is time she should be taught her place. If we could only manage to inflict some decided snub on her, she might take the hint and give up trying to poke herself in where she doesn't belong. The idea of her consenting to be elected on the freshmen executive! But she seems impervious to snubs."

"Edna, let's play a joke on her. It will serve her right. Let us send an invitation in somebody's name to the senior 'prom.'"

"The very thing! And sign Sidney Hill's name to it. He's the handsomest and richest fellows at Payzant, and belongs to one of the best families in town, and he's awfully fastidious besides. No doubt she will feel immensely flattered and, of course, she'll accept. Just think how silly she'll feel when she finds out he never sent it. Let's write it now, and send it at once. There is no time to lose, for the 'prom' is on Thursday night."

The freshmen co-eds at Payzant College did not like Grace Seeley—that is to say, the majority of them. They were a decidedly snobbish class that year. No one could deny that Grace was clever, but she was poor, dressed very plainly—"dowdily," the girls said—and "roomed" herself, that phrase meaning that she rented a little unfurnished room and cooked her own meals over an oil stove.

The "senior prom," as it was called, was the annual reception which the senior class gave in the middle of every autumn term. It was the smartest and gayest of all the college functions, and a Payzant co-ed who received an invitation to it counted herself fortunate. The senior girls were included as a matter of course, but a junior, soph, or freshie could not go unless one of the senior boys invited her.

Grace Seeley was studying Greek in her tiny room that afternoon when the invitation was brought to her. It was scrupulously orthodox in appearance and form, and Grace never doubted that it was genuine, although she felt much surprised that Sidney Hill, the leader of his class and the foremost figure in all college sports and societies, should have asked her to go with him to the senior prom.

But she was girlishly pleased at the prospect. She was as fond of a good time as any other girl, and she had secretly wished very much that she could go to the brilliant and much talked about senior prom.

Grace was quite unaware of her own unpopularity among her class co-eds, although she thought it was very hard to get acquainted with them. Without any false pride herself, and of a frank, independent nature, it never occurred to her that the other Payzant freshies could look down on her because she was poor, or resent her presence among them because she dressed plainly.

She straightway wrote a note of acceptance to Sidney Hill, and that young man naturally felt much mystified when he opened and read it in the college library next morning.

"Grace Seeley," he pondered. "That's the jolly girl with the brown eyes that I met at the philomathic the other night. She thanks me for my invitation to the senior prom, and accepts with pleasure. Why, I certainly never invited her or anyone else to go with me to the senior prom. There must be some mistake."

Grace passed him at this moment on her way to the Latin classroom. She bowed and smiled in a friendly fashion and Sidney Hill felt decidedly uncomfortable. What was he to do? He did not like to think of putting Miss Seeley in a false position because somebody had sent her an invitation in his name.

"I suppose it is some cad who has a spite at me that has done it," he reflected, "but if so I'll spoil his game. I'll take Miss Seeley to the prom as if I had never intended doing anything else. She shan't be humiliated just because there is someone at Payzant who would stoop to that sort of thing."

So he walked up the hall with Grace and expressed his pleasure at her acceptance, and on the evening of the prom he sent her a bouquet of white carnations, whose spicy fragrance reminded her of her own little garden at home. Grace thought it extremely nice of him, and dressed in a flutter of pleasant anticipation.

Her gown was a very simple one of sheer white organdie, and was the only evening dress she had. She knew there would be many smarter dresses at the reception, but the knowledge did not disturb her sensible head in the least.

She fingered the dainty white frills lovingly as she remembered the sunny summer days at home in the little sewing-room, where cherry boughs poked their blossoms in at the window, when her mother and sisters had helped her to make it, with laughing prophesies and speculations as to its first appearance. Into seam and puff and frill many girlish hopes and dreams had been sewn, and they all came back to Grace as she put it on, and helped to surround her with an atmosphere of happiness.

When she was ready she picked up her bouquet and looked herself over in the mirror, from the top of her curly head to the tips of her white shoes, with a little nod of satisfaction. Grace was not exactly pretty, but she had such a bright, happy face and such merry brown eyes and such a friendly smile that she was very pleasant to look upon, and a great many people thought so that night.

Grace had never in all her life before had so good a time as she had at that senior prom. The seniors were quick to discover her unaffected originality and charm, and everywhere she went she was the centre of a merry group. In short, Grace, as much to her own surprise as anyone's, found herself a social success.

Presently Sidney brought his brother up to be introduced, and the latter said:

"Miss Seeley, will you excuse my asking if you have a brother or any relative named Max Seeley?"

Grace nodded. "Oh, yes, my brother Max. He is a doctor out west."

"I was sure of it," said Murray Hill triumphantly. "You resemble him so strongly. Please don't consider me as a stranger a minute longer, for Max and I are like brothers. Indeed, I owe my life to him. Last summer I was out there on a surveying expedition, and I took typhoid in a little out-of-the-way place where good nursing was not to be had for love or money. Your brother attended me and he managed to pull me through. He never left me day or night until I was out of danger, and he worked like a Trojan for me."

"Dear old Max," said Grace, her brown eyes shining with pride and pleasure. "That is so like him. He is such a dear brother and I haven't seen him for four years. To see somebody who knows him so well is next best thing to seeing himself."

"He is an awfully fine fellow," said Mr. Hill heartily, "and I'm delighted to have met the 'little sister' he used to talk so much about. I want you to come ever and meet my mother and sister. They have heard me talk so much about Max that they think almost as much of him as I do, and they will be glad to meet his sister."

Mrs. Hill, a handsome, dignified lady who was one of the chaperones of the prom, received Grace warmly, while Beatrice Hill, an extremely pretty, smartly gowned girl, made her feel at home immediately.

"You came with Sid, didn't you?" she whispered. "Sid is so sly—he never tells us whom he is going to take anywhere. But when I saw you come in with him I knew I was going to like you, you looked so jolly. And you're really the sister of that splendid Dr. Seeley who saved Murray's life last summer? And to think you've been at Payzant nearly a whole term and we never knew it!"

"Well, how have you enjoyed our prom, Miss Seeley?" asked Sid, as they walked home together under the arching elms of the college campus.

"Oh! it was splendid," said Grace enthusiastically. "Everybody was so nice. And then to meet someone who could tell me so much about Max! I must write them home all about it before I sleep, just to calm my head a bit. Mother and the girls will be so interested, and I must send Lou and Mab a carnation apiece for their scrapbooks."

"Give me one back, please," said Sid. And Grace with a little blush, did so.

That night, while Grace was slipping the stems of her carnations and putting them into water, three little bits of conversation were being carried on which it is necessary to report in order to round up this story neatly and properly, as all stories should be rounded up.

In the first place, Beatrice Hill was saying to Sidney, "Oh, Sid, that Miss Seeley you had at the prom is a lovely girl. I don't know when I've met anyone I liked so much. She was so jolly and friendly and she didn't put on learned airs at all, as so many of those Payzant girls do. I asked her all about herself and she told me, and all about her mother and sisters and home and the lovely times they had together, and how hard they worked to send her to college too, and how she taught school in vacations and 'roomed' herself to help along. Isn't it so brave and plucky of her! I know we are going to be great friends."

"I hope so," said Sidney briefly, "because I have an idea that she and I are going to be very good friends too."

And Sidney went upstairs and put away a single white carnation very carefully.

In the second place, Mrs. Hill was saying to her eldest son, "I liked that

Miss Seeley very much. She seemed a very sweet girl."

And, finally, Agnes Walters and Edna Hayden were discussing the matter in great mystification in their room.

"I can't understand it at all," said Agnes slowly. "Sid Hill took her to the prom and he must have sent her those carnations too. She could never have afforded them herself. And did you see the fuss his people made over her? I heard Beatrice telling her that she was coming to call on her tomorrow, and Mrs. Hill said she must look upon 'Beechlawn' as her second home while she was at Payzant. If the Hills are going to take her up we'll have to be nice to her."

"I suppose," said Edna conclusively, "the truth of the matter is that Sid Hill meant to ask her anyway. I dare say he asked her long ago, and she would know our invitation was a fraud. So the joke is on ourselves, after all."

But, as you and I know, that, with the exception of the last sentence, was not the truth of the matter at all.

The Penningtons' Girl

Winslow had been fishing—or pretending to—all the morning, and he was desperately thirsty. He boarded with the Beckwiths on the Riverside East Shore, but he was nearer Riverside West, and he knew the Penningtons well. He had often been there for bait and milk and had listened times out of mind to Mrs. Pennington's dismal tales of her tribulations with hired girls. She never could get along with them, and they left, on an average, after a fortnight's trial. She was on the lookout for one now, he knew, and would likely be cross, but he thought she would give him a drink.

He rowed his skiff into the shore and tied it to a fir that hung out from the bank. A winding little footpath led up to the Pennington farmhouse, which crested the hill about three hundred yards from the shore. Winslow made for the kitchen door and came face to face with a girl carrying a pail of water—Mrs. Pennington's latest thing in hired girls, of course.

Winslow's first bewildered thought was "What a goddess!" and he wondered, as he politely asked for a drink, where on earth Mrs. Pennington had picked her up. She handed him a shining dipper half full and stood, pail in hand, while he drank it.

She was rather tall, and wore a somewhat limp, faded print gown, and a big sunhat, beneath which a glossy knot of chestnut showed itself. Her skin was very fair, somewhat freckled, and her mouth was delicious. As for her eyes, they were grey, but beyond that simply defied description.

"Will you have some more?" she asked in a soft, drawling voice.

"No, thank you. That was delicious. Is Mrs. Pennington home?"

"No. She has gone away for the day."

"Well, I suppose I can sit down here and rest a while. You've no serious objections, have you?"

"Oh, no."

She carried her pail into the kitchen and came out again presently with a knife and a pan of apples. Sitting down on a bench under the poplars she proceeded to peel them with a disregard of his presence that piqued Winslow, who was not used to being ignored in this fashion. Besides, as a general rule, he had been quite good friends with Mrs. Pennington's hired girls. She had had three strapping damsels during his sojourn in Riverside, and he used to sit on this very doorstep and chaff them. They had all been saucy and talkative. This girl was evidently a new species.

"Do you think you'll get along with Mrs. Pennington?" he asked finally. "As a rule she fights with her help, although she is a most estimable woman."

The girl smiled quite broadly.

"I guess p'r'aps she's rather hard to suit," was the answer, "but I like her pretty well so far. I think we'll get along with each other. If we don't I can leave—like the others did."

"What is your name?"

"Nelly Ray."

"Well, Nelly, I hope you'll be able to keep your place. Let me give you a bit of friendly advice. Don't let the cats get into the pantry. That is what Mrs. Pennington has quarrelled with nearly every one of her girls about."

"It is quite a bother to keep them out, ain't it?" said Nelly calmly. "There's dozens of cats about the place. What on earth makes them keep so many?"

"Mr. Pennington has a mania for cats. He and Mrs. Pennington have a standing disagreement about it. The last girl left here because she couldn't stand the cats; they affected her nerves, she said. I hope you don't mind them."

"Oh, no; I kind of like cats. I've been tryin' to count them. Has anyone ever done that?"

"Not that I know of. I tried but I had to give up in despair—never could tell when I was counting the same cat over again. Look at that black goblin sunning himself on the woodpile. I say, Nelly, you're not going, are you?"

"I must. It's time to get dinner. Mr. Pennington will be in from the fields soon."

The next minute he heard her stepping briskly about the kitchen, shooing out intruding cats, and humming a darky air to herself. He went reluctantly back to the shore and rowed across the river in a brown study.

I don't know whether Winslow was afflicted with chronic thirst or not, or whether the East side water wasn't so good as that of the West side; but I do know that he fairly haunted the Pennington farmhouse after that. Mrs. Pennington was home the next time he went, and he asked her about her new girl. To his surprise the good lady was unusually reticent. She couldn't really say very much about Nelly. No, she didn't belong anywhere near Riverside. In fact, she—Mrs. Pennington—didn't think she had any settled home at present. Her father was travelling over the country somewhere. Nelly was a good little girl, and very obliging. Beyond this Winslow could get no more information, so he went around and talked to Nelly, who was sitting on the bench under the poplars and seemed absorbed in watching the sunset.

She dropped her g's badly and made some grammatical errors that caused Winslow's flesh to creep on his bones. But any man could have forgiven mistakes from such dimpled lips in such a sweet voice.

He asked her to go for a row up the river in the twilight and she assented; she handled an oar very well, he found out, and the exercise became her. Winslow tried to get her to talk about herself, but failed signally and had to content himself with Mrs. Pennington's meagre information. He told her about himself frankly enough—how he had had fever in the spring and had been ordered to spend the summer in the country and do nothing useful until his health was fully restored, and how lonesome it was in Riverside in general and at the Beckwith farm in particular. He made out quite a dismal case for himself and if Nelly wasn't sorry for him, she should have been.

At the end of a fortnight Riverside folks began to talk about Winslow and the Penningtons' hired girl. He was reported to be "dead gone" on her; he took her out rowing every evening, drove her to preaching up the Bend on Sunday nights, and haunted the Pennington farmhouse. Wise folks shook their heads over it and wondered that Mrs. Pennington allowed it. Winslow was a gentleman, and that Nelly Ray, whom nobody knew anything about, not even where she came from, was only a common hired girl, and he had no business to be hanging about her. She was pretty, to be sure; but she was absurdly stuck-up and wouldn't associate with other Riverside "help" at all. Well, pride must have a fall; there must be something queer about her when she was so awful sly as to her past life.

Winslow and Nelly did not trouble themselves in the least over all this gossip; in fact, they never even heard it. Winslow was hopelessly in love, when he found this out he was aghast. He thought of his father, the ambitious railroad magnate; of his mother, the brilliant society leader; of his sisters, the beautiful and proud; he was honestly frightened. It would never do; he must not go to see Nelly again. He kept this prudent resolution for twenty-four hours and then rowed over to the West shore. He found Nelly sitting on the bank in her old faded print dress and he straightway forgot everything he ought to have remembered.

Nelly herself never seemed to be conscious of the social gulf between them. At least she never alluded to it in any way, and accepted Winslow's attentions as if she had a perfect right to them. She had broken the record by staying with Mrs. Pennington four weeks, and even the cats were in subjection.

Winslow was well enough to have gone back to the city and, in fact, his father was writing for him. But he couldn't leave Beckwiths', apparently. At any rate he stayed on and met Nelly every day and cursed himself for a cad and a cur and a weak-brained idiot.

One day he took Nelly for a row up the river. They went further than usual around the Bend. Winslow didn't want to go too far, for he knew that a party of his city friends, chaperoned by Mrs. Keyton-Wells, were having a picnic somewhere up along the river shore that day. But Nelly insisted on going on and on, and of course she had her way. When they reached a little pine-fringed headland they came upon the picnickers, within a stone's throw. Everybody recognized Winslow. "Why, there is Burton!" he heard Mrs. Keyton-Wells exclaim, and he knew she was putting up her glasses. Will Evans, who was an especial chum of his, ran down to the water's edge. "Bless me, Win, where did you come from? Come right in. We haven't had tea yet. Bring your friend too," he added, becoming conscious that Winslow's friend was a mighty pretty girl. Winslow's face was crimson. He avoided Nelly's eye.

"Are them people friends of yours?" she asked in a low tone.

"Yes," he muttered.

"Well, let us go ashore if they want us to," she said calmly. "I don't mind."

For three seconds Winslow hesitated. Then he pulled ashore and helped Nelly to alight on a jutting rock. There was a curious, set expression about his fine mouth as he marched Nelly up to Mrs. Keyton-Wells and introduced her. Mrs. Keyton-Wells's greeting was slightly cool, but very polite. She supposed Miss Ray was some little country girl with whom Burton Winslow was carrying on a summer flirtation; respectable enough, no doubt, and must be treated civilly, but of course wouldn't expect to be made an equal of exactly. The other women took their cue from her, but the men were more cordial. Miss Ray might be shabby, but she was distinctly fetching, and Winslow looked savage.

Nelly was not a whit abashed, seemingly, by the fashionable circle in which she found herself, and she talked away to Will Evans and the others in her soft drawl as if she had known them all her life. All might have gone passably well, had not a little Riverside imp, by name of Rufus Hent, who had been picked up by the picnickers to run their errands, come up just then with a pail of water.

"Golly!" he ejaculated in very audible tones. "If there ain't Mrs. Pennington's hired girl!"

Mrs. Keyton-Wells stiffened with horror. Winslow darted a furious glance at the tell-tale that would have annihilated anything except a small boy. Will Evans grinned and went on talking to Nelly, who had failed to hear, or at least to heed, the exclamation.

The mischief was done, the social thermometer went down to zero in Nelly's neighbourhood. The women ignored her altogether. Winslow set his teeth together and registered a mental vow to wring Rufus Hent's sunburned neck at the first opportunity. He escorted Nelly to the table and waited on her with ostentatious deference, while Mrs. Keyton-Wells glanced at him stonily and made up her mind to tell his mother when she went home.

Nelly's social ostracism did not affect her appetite. But after lunch was over, she walked down to the skiff. Winslow followed her.

"Do you want to go home?" he asked.

"Yes, it's time I went, for the cats may be raidin' the pantry. But you must not come; your friends here want you."

"Nonsense!" said Winslow sulkily. "If you are going I am too."

But Nelly was too quick for him; she sprang into the skiff, unwound the rope, and pushed off before he guessed her intention.

"I can row myself home and I mean to," she announced, taking up the oars defiantly.

"Nelly," he implored.

Nelly looked at him wickedly.

"You'd better go back to your friends. That old woman with the eyeglasses is watchin' you."

Winslow said something strong under his breath as he went back to the others. Will Evans and his chums began to chaff him about Nelly, but he looked so dangerous that they concluded to stop. There is no denying that Winslow was in a fearful temper just then with Mrs. Keyton-Wells, Evans, himself, Nelly—in fact, with all the world.

His friends drove him home in the evening on their way to the station and dropped him at the Beckwith farm. At dusk he went moodily down to the shore. Far up the Bend was dim and shadowy and stars were shining above the wooded shores. Over the river the Pennington farmhouse lights twinkled out alluringly. Winslow watched them until he could stand it no longer. Nelly had made off with his skiff, but Perry Beckwith's dory was ready to hand. In five minutes, Winslow was grounding her on the West shore. Nelly was sitting on a rock at the landing place. He went over and sat down silently beside her. A full moon was rising above the dark hills up the Bend and in the faint light the girl was wonderfully lovely.

"I thought you weren't comin' over at all tonight," she said, smiling up at him, "and I was sorry, because I wanted to say goodbye to you."

"Goodbye? Nelly, you're not going away?"

"Yes. The cats were in the pantry when I got home."

"Nelly!"

"Well, to be serious. I'm not goin' for that, but I really am goin'. I had a letter from Dad this evenin'. Did you have a good time after I left this afternoon? Did Mrs. Keyton-Wells thaw out?"

"Hang Mrs. Keyton-Wells! Nelly, where are you going?"

"To Dad, of course. We used to live down south together, but two months ago we broke up housekeepin' and come north. We thought we could do better up here, you know. Dad started out to look for a place to settle down and I came here while he was prospectin'. He's got a house now, he says, and wants me to go right off. I'm goin' tomorrow."

"Nelly, you mustn't go—you mustn't, I tell you," exclaimed Winslow in despair. "I love you—I love you—you must stay with me forever."

"You don't know what you're sayin', Mr. Winslow," said Nelly coldly. "Why, you can't marry me—a common servant girl."

"I can and I will, if you'll have me," answered Winslow recklessly. "I can't ever let you go. I've loved you ever since I first saw you. Nelly, won't you be my wife? Don't you love me?"

"Well, yes, I do," confessed Nelly suddenly; and then it was fully five minutes before Winslow gave her a chance to say anything else.

"Oh, what will your people say?" she contrived to ask at last. "Won't they be in a dreadful state? Oh, it will never do for you to marry me."

"Won't it?" said Winslow in a tone of satisfaction. "I rather think it will. Of course, my family will rampage a bit at first. I daresay Father'll turn me out. Don't worry over that, Nelly. I'm not afraid of work. I'm not afraid of anything except losing you."

"You'll have to see what Dad says," remarked Nelly, after another eloquent interlude.

"He won't object, will he? I'll write to him or go and see him. Where is he?"

"He is in town at the Arlington."

"The Arlington!" Winslow was amazed. The Arlington was the most exclusive and expensive hotel in town.

"What is he doing there?"

"Transacting a real estate or railroad deal with your father, I believe, or something of that sort."

"Nelly!"

"Well?"

"What do you mean?"

"Just what I say."

Winslow got up and looked at her.

"Nelly, who are you?"

"Helen Ray Scott, at your service, sir."

"Not Helen Ray Scott, the daughter of the railroad king?"

"The same. Are you sorry that you're engaged to her? If you are, she'll stay Nelly Ray."

Winslow dropped back on the seat with a long breath.

"Nelly, I don't understand. Why did you deceive me? I feel stunned."

"Oh, do forgive me," she said merrily. "I shouldn't have, I suppose—but you know you took me for the hired girl the very first time you saw me, and you patronized me and called me Nelly; so I let you think so just for fun. I never thought it would come to this. When Father and I came north I took a fancy to come here and stay with Mrs. Pennington—who is an old nurse of mine—until Father decided where to take up our abode. I got here the night before we met. My trunk was delayed so I put on an old cotton dress her niece had left here—and you came and saw me. I made Mrs. Pennington keep the secret—she thought it great fun; and I really was a great hand to do little chores and keep the cats in subjection too. I made mistakes in grammar and dropped my g's on purpose—it was such fun to see you wince when I did it. It was cruel to tease you so, I suppose, but it was so sweet just to be loved for myself—not because I was an heiress and a belle—I couldn't bear to tell you the truth. Did you think I couldn't read your thoughts this afternoon, when I insisted on going ashore? You were a little ashamed of me—you know you were. I didn't blame you for that, but if you hadn't gone ashore and taken me as you did I would never have spoken to you again. Mrs. Keyton-Wells won't snub me next time we meet. And some way I don't think your father will turn you out, either. Have you forgiven me yet, Burton?"

"I shall never call you anything but Nelly," said Winslow irrelevantly.

The Red Room

You would have me tell you the story, Grandchild? 'Tis a sad one and best forgotten—few remember it now. There are always sad and dark stories in old families such as ours.

Yet I have promised and must keep my word. So sit down here at my feet and rest your bright head on my lap, that I may not see in your young eyes the shadows my story will bring across their bonny blue.

I was a mere child when it all happened, yet I remember it but too well, and I can recall how pleased I was when my father's stepmother, Mrs. Montressor—she not liking to be called grandmother, seeing she was but turned of fifty and a handsome woman still—wrote to my mother that she must send little Beatrice up to Montressor Place for the Christmas holidays. So I went joyfully though my mother grieved to part with me; she had little to love save me, my father, Conrad Montressor, having been lost at sea when but three months wed.

My aunts were wont to tell me how much I resembled him, being, so they said, a Montressor to the backbone; and this I took to mean commendation, for the Montressors were a well-descended and well-thought-of family, and the women were noted for their beauty. This I could well believe, since of all my aunts there was not one but was counted a pretty woman. Therefore I took heart of grace when I thought of my dark face and spindling shape, hoping that when I should be grown up I might be counted not unworthy of my race.

The Place was an old-fashioned, mysterious house, such as I delighted in, and Mrs. Montressor was ever kind to me, albeit a little stern, for she was a proud woman and cared but little for children, having none of her own.

But there were books there to pore over without let or hindrance—for nobody questioned of my whereabouts if I but kept out of the way—and strange, dim family portraits on the walls to gaze upon, until I knew each proud old face well, and had visioned a history for it in my own mind—for I was given to dreaming and was older and wiser than my years, having no childish companions to keep me still a child.

There were always some of my aunts at the Place to kiss and make much of me for my father's sake—for he had been their favourite brother. My aunts —there were eight of them—had all married well, so said people who knew, and lived not far away, coming home often to take tea with Mrs. Montressor, who had always gotten on well with her step-daughters, or to help prepare for some festivity or other—for they were notable housekeepers, every one.

They were all at Montressor Place for Christmas, and I got more petting than I deserved, albeit they looked after me somewhat more strictly than did Mrs. Montressor, and saw to it that I did not read too many fairy tales or sit up later at nights than became my years.

But it was not for fairy tales and sugarplums nor yet for petting that I rejoiced to be at the Place at that time. Though I spoke not of it to anyone, I had a great longing to see my Uncle Hugh's wife, concerning whom I had heard much, both good and bad.

My Uncle Hugh, albeit the oldest of the family, had never married until now, and all the countryside rang with talk of his young wife. I did not hear as much as I wished, for the gossips took heed to my presence when I drew anear and turned to other matters. Yet, being somewhat keener of comprehension than they knew, I heard and understood not a little of their talk.

And so I came to know that neither proud Mrs. Montressor nor my good aunts, nor even my gentle mother, looked with overmuch favour on what my Uncle Hugh had done. And I did hear that Mrs. Montressor had chosen a wife for her stepson, of good family and some beauty, but that my Uncle Hugh would have none of her—a thing Mrs. Montressor found hard to pardon, yet might so have done had not my uncle, on his last voyage to the Indies—for he went often in his own vessels—married and brought home a foreign bride, of whom no one knew aught save that her beauty was a thing to dazzle the day and that she was of some strange alien blood such as ran not in the blue veins of the Montressors.

Some had much to say of her pride and insolence, and wondered if Mrs. Montressor would tamely yield her mistress-ship to the stranger. But others, who were taken with her loveliness and grace, said that the tales told were born of envy and malice, and that Alicia Montressor was well worthy of her name and station.

So I halted between two opinions and thought to judge for myself, but when I went to the Place my Uncle Hugh and his bride were gone for a time, and I had even to swallow my disappointment and bide their return with all my small patience.

But my aunts and their stepmother talked much of Alicia, and they spoke slightingly of her, saying that she was but a light woman and that no good would come of my Uncle Hugh's having wed her, with other things of a like nature. Also they spoke of the company she gathered around her, thinking her to have strange and unbecoming companions for a Montressor. All this I heard and pondered much over, although my good aunts supposed that such a chit as I would take no heed to their whisperings.

When I was not with them, helping to whip eggs and stone raisins, and being watched to see that I ate not more than one out of five, I was surely to be found in the wing hall, poring over my book and grieving that I was no more allowed to go into the Red Room.

The wing hall was a narrow one and dim, connecting the main rooms of the Place with an older wing, built in a curious way. The hall was lighted by small, square-paned windows, and at its end a little flight of steps led up to the Red Room.

Whenever I had been at the Place before—and this was often—I had passed much of my time in this same Red Room. It was Mrs. Montressor's sitting-room then, where she wrote her letters and examined household accounts, and sometimes had an old gossip in to tea. The room was low-ceilinged and dim, hung with red damask, and with odd, square windows high up under the eaves and a dark wainscoting all around it. And there I loved to sit quietly on the red sofa and read my fairy tales, or talk dreamily to the swallows fluttering crazily against the tiny panes.

When I had gone this Christmas to the Place I soon bethought myself of the Red Room—for I had a great love for it. But I had got no further than the steps when Mrs. Montressor came sweeping down the hall in haste and, catching me by the arm, pulled me back as roughly as if it had been Bluebeard's chamber itself into which I was venturing.

Then, seeing my face, which I doubt not was startled enough, she seemed to repent of her haste and patted me gently on the head.

"There, there, little Beatrice! Did I frighten you, child? Forgive an old woman's thoughtlessness. But be not too ready to go where you are not bidden, and never venture foot in the Red Room now, for it belongs to your Uncle Hugh's wife, and let me tell you she is not over fond of intruders."

I felt sorry overmuch to hear this, nor could I see why my new aunt should care if I went in once in a while, as had been my habit, to talk to the swallows and misplace nothing. But Mrs. Montressor saw to it that I obeyed her, and I went no more to the Red Room, but busied myself with other matters.

For there were great doings at the Place and much coming and going. My aunts were never idle; there was to be much festivity Christmas week and a ball on Christmas Eve. And my aunts had promised me—though not till I had wearied them of my coaxing—that I should stay up that night and see as much of the gaiety as was good for me. So I did their errands and went early to bed every night without complaint—though I did this the more readily for that, when they thought me safely asleep, they would come in and talk around my bedroom fire, saying that of Alicia which I should not have heard.

At last came the day when my Uncle Hugh and his wife were expected home—though not until my scanty patience was well nigh wearied out—and we were all assembled to meet them in the great hall, where a ruddy firelight was gleaming.

My Aunt Frances had dressed me in my best white frock and my crimson sash, with much lamenting over my skinny neck and arms, and bade me behave prettily, as became my bringing up. So I slipped in a corner, my hands and feet cold with excitement, for I think every drop of blood in my body had gone to my head, and my heart beat so hardly that it even pained me.

Then the door opened and Alicia—for so I was used to hearing her called, nor did I ever think of her as my aunt in my own mind—came in, and a little in the rear my tall, dark uncle.

She came proudly forward to the fire and stood there superbly while she loosened her cloak, nor did she see me at all at first, but nodded, a little disdainfully, it seemed, to Mrs. Montressor and my aunts, who were grouped about the drawing-room door, very ladylike and quiet.

But I neither saw nor heard aught at the time save her only, for her beauty, when she came forth from her crimson cloak and hood, was something so wonderful that I forgot my manners and stared at her as one fascinated—as indeed I was, for never had I seen such loveliness and hardly dreamed it.

Pretty women I had seen in plenty, for my aunts and my mother were counted fair, but my uncle's wife was as little like to them as a sunset glow to pale moonshine or a crimson rose to white day-lilies.

Nor can I paint her to you in words as I saw her then, with the long tongues of firelight licking her white neck and wavering over the rich masses of her red-gold hair.

She was tall—so tall that my aunts looked but insignificant beside her, and they were of no mean height, as became their race; yet no queen could have carried herself more royally, and all the passion and fire of her foreign nature burned in her splendid eyes, that might have been dark or light for aught that I could ever tell, but which seemed always like pools of warm flame, now tender, now fierce.

Her skin was like a delicate white rose leaf, and when she spoke I told my foolish self that never had I heard music before; nor do I ever again think to hear a voice so sweet, so liquid, as that which rippled over her ripe lips.

I had often in my own mind pictured this, my first meeting with Alicia, now in one way, now in another, but never had I dreamed of her speaking to me at all, so that it came to me as a great surprise when she turned and, holding out her lovely hands, said very graciously:

"And is this the little Beatrice? I have heard much of you—come, kiss me, child."

And I went, despite my Aunt Elizabeth's black frown, for the glamour of her loveliness was upon me, and I no longer wondered that my Uncle Hugh should have loved her.

Very proud of her was he too; yet I felt, rather than saw—for I was sensitive and quick of perception, as old-young children ever are—that there was something other than pride and love in his face when he looked on her, and more in his manner than the fond lover—as it were, a sort of lurking mistrust.

Nor could I think, though to me the thought seemed as treason, that she loved her husband overmuch, for she seemed half condescending and half disdainful to him; yet one thought not of this in her presence, but only remembered it when she had gone.

When she went out it seemed to me that nothing was left, so I crept lonesomely away to the wing hall and sat down by a window to dream of her; and she filled my thoughts so fully that it was no surprise when I raised my eyes and saw her coming down the hall alone, her bright head shining against the dark old walls.

When she paused by me and asked me lightly of what I was dreaming, since I had such a sober face, I answered her truly that it was of her—whereat she laughed, as one not ill pleased, and said half mockingly:

"Waste not your thoughts so, little Beatrice. But come with me, child, if you will, for I have taken a strange fancy to your solemn eyes. Perchance the warmth of your young life may thaw out the ice that has frozen around my heart ever since I came among these cold Montressors."

And, though I understood not her meaning, I went, glad to see the Red Room once more. So she made me sit down and talk to her, which I did, for shyness was no failing of mine; and she asked me many questions, and some that I thought she should not have asked, but I could not answer them, so 'twere little harm.

After that I spent a part of every day with her in the Red Room. And my Uncle Hugh was there often, and he would kiss her and praise her loveliness, not heeding my presence—for I was but a child.

Yet it ever seemed to me that she endured rather than welcomed his caresses, and at times the ever-burning flame in her eyes glowed so luridly that a chill dread would creep over me, and I would remember what my Aunt Elizabeth had said, she being a bitter-tongued woman, though kind at heart—that this strange creature would bring on us all some evil fortune yet.

Then would I strive to banish such thoughts and chide myself for doubting one so kind to me.

When Christmas Eve drew nigh my silly head was full of the ball day and night. But a grievous disappointment befell me, for I awakened that day very ill with a most severe cold; and though I bore me bravely, my aunts discovered it soon, when, despite my piteous pleadings, I was put to bed, where I cried bitterly and would not be comforted. For I thought I should not see the fine folk and, more than all, Alicia.

But that disappointment, at least, was spared me, for at night she came into my room, knowing of my longing—she was ever indulgent to my little wishes. And when I saw her I forgot my aching limbs and burning brow, and even the ball I was not to see, for never was mortal creature so lovely as she, standing there by my bed.

Her gown was of white, and there was nothing I could liken the stuff to save moonshine falling athwart a frosted pane, and out from it swelled her gleaming breast and arms, so bare that it seemed to me a shame to look upon them. Yet it could not be denied they were of wondrous beauty, white as polished marble.

And all about her snowy throat and rounded arms, and in the masses of her splendid hair, were sparkling, gleaming stones, with hearts of pure light, which I know now to have been diamonds, but knew not then, for never had I seen aught of their like.

And I gazed at her, drinking in her beauty until my soul was filled, as she stood like some goddess before her worshipper. I think she read my thought in my face and liked it—for she was a vain woman, and to such even the admiration of a child is sweet.

Then she leaned down to me until her splendid eyes looked straight into my dazzled ones.

"Tell me, little Beatrice—for they say the word of a child is to be believed—tell me, do you think me beautiful?"

I found my voice and told her truly that I thought her beautiful beyond my dreams of angels—as indeed she was. Whereat she smiled as one well pleased.

Then my Uncle Hugh came in, and though I thought that his face darkened as he looked on the naked splendour of her breast and arms, as if he liked not that the eyes of other men should gloat on it, yet he kissed her with all a lover's fond pride, while she looked at him half mockingly.

Then said he, "Sweet, will you grant me a favour?"

And she answered, "It may be that I will."

And he said, "Do not dance with that man tonight, Alicia. I mistrust him much."

His voice had more of a husband's command than a lover's entreaty. She looked at him with some scorn, but when she saw his face grow black—for the Montressors brooked scant disregard of their authority, as I had good reason to know—she seemed to change, and a smile came to her lips, though her eyes glowed balefully.

Then she laid her arms about his neck and—though it seemed to me that she had as soon strangled as embraced him—her voice was wondrous sweet and caressing as she murmured in his ear.

He laughed and his brow cleared, though he said still sternly, "Do not try me too far, Alicia."

Then they went out, she a little in advance and very stately.

After that my aunts also came in, very beautifully and modestly dressed, but they seemed to me as nothing after Alicia. For I was caught in the snare of her beauty, and the longing to see her again so grew upon me that after a time I did an undutiful and disobedient thing.

I had been straitly charged to stay in bed, which I did not, but got up and put on a gown. For it was in my mind to go quietly down, if by chance I might again see Alicia, myself unseen.

But when I reached the great hall I heard steps approaching and, having a guilty conscience, I slipped aside into the blue parlour and hid me behind the curtains lest my aunts should see me.

Then Alicia came in, and with her a man whom I had never before seen. Yet I instantly bethought myself of a lean black snake, with a glittering and evil eye, which I had seen in Mrs. Montressor's garden two summers agone, and which was like to have bitten me. John, the gardener, had killed it, and I verily thought that if it had a soul, it must have gotten into this man.

Alicia sat down and he beside her, and when he had put his arms about her, he kissed her face and lips. Nor did she shrink from his embrace, but even smiled and leaned nearer to him with a little smooth motion, as they talked to each other in some strange, foreign tongue.

I was but a child and innocent, nor knew I aught of honour and dishonour. Yet it seemed to me that no man should kiss her save only my Uncle Hugh, and from that hour I mistrusted Alicia, though I understood not then what I afterwards did.

And as I watched them—not thinking of playing the spy—I saw her face grow suddenly cold, and she straightened herself up and pushed away her lover's arms.

Then I followed her guilty eyes to the door, where stood my Uncle Hugh, and all the pride and passion of the Montressors sat on his lowering brow. Yet he came forward quietly as Alicia and the snake drew apart and stood up.

At first he looked not at his guilty wife but at her lover, and smote him heavily in the face. Whereat he, being a coward at heart, as are all villains, turned white and slunk from the room with a muttered oath, nor was he stayed.

My uncle turned to Alicia, and very calmly and terribly he said, "From this hour you are no longer wife of mine!"

And there was that in his tone which told that his forgiveness and love should be hers nevermore.

Then he motioned her out and she went, like a proud queen, with her glorious head erect and no shame on her brow.

As for me, when they were gone I crept away, dazed and bewildered enough, and went back to my bed, having seen and heard more than I had a mind for, as disobedient people and eavesdroppers ever do.

But my Uncle Hugh kept his word, and Alicia was no more wife to him, save only in name. Yet of gossip or scandal there was none, for the pride of his race kept secret his dishonour, nor did he ever seem other than a courteous and respectful husband.

Nor did Mrs. Montressor and my aunts, though they wondered much among themselves, learn aught, for they dared question neither their brother nor Alicia, who carried herself as loftily as ever, and seemed to pine for neither lover nor husband. As for me, no one dreamed I knew aught of it, and I kept my own counsel as to what I had seen in the blue parlour on the night of the Christmas ball.

After the New Year I went home, but ere long Mrs. Montressor sent for me again, saying that the house was lonely without little Beatrice. So I went again and found all unchanged, though the Place was very quiet, and Alicia went out but little from the Red Room.

Of my Uncle Hugh I saw little, save when he went and came on the business of his estate, somewhat more gravely and silently than of yore, or brought to me books and sweetmeats from town.

But every day I was with Alicia in the Red Room, where she would talk to me, oftentimes wildly and strangely, but always kindly. And though I think Mrs. Montressor liked our intimacy none too well, she said no word, and I came and went as I listed with Alicia, though never quite liking her strange ways and the restless fire in her eyes.

Nor would I ever kiss her, after I had seen her lips pressed by the snake's, though she sometimes coaxed me, and grew pettish and vexed when I would not; but she guessed not my reason.

March came in that year like a lion, exceedingly hungry and fierce, and my Uncle Hugh had ridden away through the storm nor thought to be back for some days.

In the afternoon I was sitting in the wing hall, dreaming wondrous day-dreams, when Alicia called me to the Red Room. And as I went, I marvelled anew at her loveliness, for the blood was leaping in her face and her jewels were dim before the lustre of her eyes. Her hand, when she took mine, was burning hot, and her voice had a strange ring.

"Come, little Beatrice," she said, "come talk to me, for I know not what to do with my lone self today. Time hangs heavily in this gloomy house. I do verily think this Red Room has an evil influence over me. See if your childish prattle can drive away the ghosts that riot in these dark old corners—ghosts of a ruined and shamed life! Nay, shrink not—do I talk wildly? I mean not all I say—my brain seems on fire, little Beatrice. Come; it may be you know some grim old legend of this room—it must surely have one. Never was place fitter for a dark deed! Tush! never be so frightened, child—forget my vagaries. Tell me now and I will listen."

Whereat she cast herself lithely on the satin couch and turned her lovely face on me. So I gathered up my small wits and told her what I was not supposed to know—how that, generations agone, a Montressor had disgraced himself and his name, and that, when he came home to his mother, she had met him in that same Red Room and flung at him taunts and reproaches, forgetting whose breast had nourished him; and that he, frantic with shame and despair, turned his sword against his own heart and so died. But his mother went mad with her remorse, and was kept a prisoner in the Red Room until her death.

So lamely told I the tale, as I had heard my Aunt Elizabeth tell it, when she knew not I listened or understood. Alicia heard me through and said nothing, save that it was a tale worthy of the Montressors. Whereat I bridled, for I too was a Montressor, and proud of it.

But she took my hand soothingly in hers and said, "Little Beatrice, if tomorrow or the next day they should tell you, those cold, proud women, that Alicia was unworthy of your love, tell me, would you believe them?"

And I, remembering what I had seen in the blue parlour, was silent—for I could not lie. So she flung my hand away with a bitter laugh, and picked lightly from the table anear a small dagger with a jewelled handle.

It seemed to me a cruel-looking toy and I said so—whereat she smiled and drew her white fingers down the thin, shining blade in a fashion that made me cold.

"Such a little blow with this," she said, "such a little blow—and the heart beats no longer, the weary brain rests, the lips and eyes smile never again! 'Twere a short path out of all difficulties, my Beatrice."

And I, understanding her not, yet shivering, begged her to cast it aside, which she did carelessly and, putting a hand under my chin, she turned up my face to hers.

"Little, grave-eyed Beatrice, tell me truly, would it grieve you much if you were never again to sit here with Alicia in this same Red Room?"

And I made answer earnestly that it would, glad that I could say so much truly. Then her face grew tender and she sighed deeply.

Presently she opened a quaint, inlaid box and took from it a shining gold chain of rare workmanship and exquisite design, and this she hung around my neck, nor would suffer me to thank her but laid her hand gently on my lips.

"Now go," she said. "But ere you leave me, little Beatrice, grant me but the one favour—it may be that I shall never ask another of you. Your people, I know—those cold Montressors—care little for me, but with all my faults, I have ever been kind to you. So, when the morrow's come, and they tell you that Alicia is as one worse than dead, think not of me with scorn only but grant me a little pity—for I was not always what I am now, and might never have become so had a little child like you been always anear me, to keep me pure and innocent. And I would have you but the once lay your arms about my neck and kiss me."

And I did so, wondering much at her manner—for it had in it a strange tenderness and some sort of hopeless longing. Then she gently put me from the room, and I sat musing by the hall window until night fell darkly—and a fearsome night it was, of storm and blackness. And I thought how well it was that my Uncle Hugh had not to return in such a tempest. Yet, ere the thought had grown cold, the door opened and he strode down the hall, his cloak drenched and wind-twisted, in one hand a whip, as though he had but then sprung from his horse, in the other what seemed like a crumpled letter.

Nor was the night blacker than his face, and he took no heed of me as I ran after him, thinking selfishly of the sweetmeats he had promised to bring me—but I thought no more of them when I got to the door of the Red Room.

Alicia stood by the table, hooded and cloaked as for a journey, but her hood had slipped back, and her face rose from it marble-white, save where her wrathful eyes burned out, with dread and guilt and hatred in their depths, while she had one arm raised as if to thrust him back.

As for my uncle, he stood before her and I saw not his face, but his voice was low and terrible, speaking words I understood not then, though long afterwards I came to know their meaning.

And he cast foul scorn at her that she should have thought to fly with her lover, and swore that naught should again thwart his vengeance, with other threats, wild and dreadful enough.

Yet she said no word until he had done, and then she spoke, but what she said I know not, save that it was full of hatred and defiance and wild accusation, such as a mad woman might have uttered.

And she defied him even then to stop her flight, though he told her to cross that threshold would mean her death; for he was a wronged and desperate man and thought of nothing save his own dishonour.

Then she made as if to pass him, but he caught her by her white wrist; she turned on him with fury, and I saw her right hand reach stealthily out over the table behind her, where lay the dagger.

"Let me go!" she hissed.

And he said, "I will not."

Then she turned herself about and struck at him with the dagger—and never saw I such a face as was hers at the moment.

He fell heavily, yet held her even in death, so that she had to wrench herself free, with a shriek that rings yet in my ears on a night when the wind wails over the rainy moors. She rushed past me unheeding, and fled down the hall like a hunted creature, and I heard the heavy door clang hollowly behind her.

As for me, I stood there looking at the dead man, for I could neither move nor speak and was like to have died of horror. And presently I knew nothing, nor did I come to my recollection for many a day, when I lay abed, sick of a fever and more like to die than live.

So that when at last I came out from the shadow of death, my Uncle Hugh had been long cold in his grave, and the hue and cry for his guilty wife was well nigh over, since naught had been seen or heard of her since she fled the country with her foreign lover.

When I came rightly to my remembrance, they questioned me as to what I had seen and heard in the Red Room. And I told them as best I could, though much aggrieved that to my questions they would answer nothing save to bid me to stay still and think not of the matter.

Then my mother, sorely vexed over my adventures—which in truth were but sorry ones for a child—took me home. Nor would she let me keep Alicia's chain, but made away with it, how I knew not and little cared, for the sight of it was loathsome to me.

It was many years ere I went again to Montressor Place, and I never saw the Red Room more, for Mrs. Montressor had the old wing torn down, deeming its sorrowful memories dark heritage enough for the next Montressor.

So, Grandchild, the sad tale is ended, and you will not see the Red Room when you go next month to Montressor Place. The swallows still build under the eaves, though—I know not if you will understand their speech as I did.

The Setness of Theodosia

When Theodosia Ford married Wesley Brooke after a courtship of three years, everybody concerned was satisfied. There was nothing particularly romantic in either the courtship or marriage. Wesley was a steady, well-meaning, rather slow fellow, comfortably off. He was not at all handsome. But Theodosia was a very pretty girl with the milky colouring of an auburn blonde and large china-blue eyes. She looked mild and Madonna-like and was known to be sweet-tempered. Wesley's older brother, Irving Brooke, had married a woman who kept him in hot water all the time, so Heatherton folks said, but they thought there was no fear of that with Wesley and Theodosia. They would get along together all right.

Only old Jim Parmelee shook his head and said, "They might, and then again they mightn't"; he knew the stock they came of and it was a kind you could never predict about.

Wesley and Theodosia were third cousins; this meant that old Henry Ford had been the great-great-grandfather of them both. Jim Parmelee, who was ninety, had been a small boy when this remote ancestor was still alive.

"I mind him well," said old Jim on the morning of Theodosia's wedding day. There was a little group about the blacksmith's forge. Old Jim was in the centre. He was a fat, twinkling-eyed old man, fresh and ruddy in spite of his ninety years. "And," he went on, "he was about the settest man you'd ever see or want to see. When old Henry Ford made up his mind on any p'int a cyclone wouldn't turn him a hairsbreadth—no, nor an earthquake neither. Didn't matter a mite how much he suffered for it—he'd stick to it if it broke his heart. There was always some story or other going round about old Henry's setness. The family weren't quite so bad—only Tom. He was Dosia's great-grandfather, and a regular chip of the old block. Since then it's cropped out now and again all through the different branches of the family. I mistrust if Dosia hasn't got a spice of it, and Wes Brooke too, but mebbe not."

Old Jim was the only croaker. Wesley and Theodosia were married, in the golden prime of the Indian summer, and settled down on their snug little farm. Dosia was a beautiful bride, and Wesley's pride in her was amusingly apparent. He thought nothing too good for her, the Heatherton people said. It was a sight to make an old heart young to see him march up the aisle of the church on Sunday in all the glossy splendour of his wedding suit, his curly black head held high and his round boyish face shining with happiness, stopping and turning proudly at his pew to show Theodosia in.

They always sat alone together in the big pew, and Alma Spencer, who sat behind them, declared that they held each other's hands all through the service. This lasted until spring; then came a sensation and scandal, such as decorous Heatherton had not known since the time Isaac Allen got drunk at Centreville Fair and came home and kicked his wife.

One evening in early April Wesley came home from the store at "the Corner," where he had lingered to talk over politics and farming methods with his cronies. This evening he was later than usual, and Theodosia had his supper kept warm for him. She met him on the porch and kissed him. He kissed her in return, and held her to him for a minute, with her bright head on his shoulder. The frogs were singing down in the south meadow swamp, and there was a splendour of silvery moonrise over the wooded Heatherton hills. Theodosia always remembered that moment.

When they went in, Wesley, full of excitement, began to talk of what he had heard at the store. Ogden Greene and Tom Cary were going to sell out and go to Manitoba. There were better chances for a man out there, he said; in Heatherton he might slave all his life and never make more than a bare living. Out west he might make a fortune.

Wesley talked on in this strain for some time, rehashing all the arguments he had heard Greene and Cary use. He had always been rather disposed to grumble at his limited chances in Heatherton, and now the great West seemed to stretch before him, full of alluring prospects and visions. Ogden and Tom wanted him to go too, he said. He had half a notion to. Heatherton was a stick-in-the-mud sort of place anyhow.

"What say, Dosia?"

He looked across the table at her, his eyes bright and questioning. Theodosia had listened in silence, as she poured his tea and passed him her hot, flaky biscuits. There was a little perpendicular wrinkle between her straight eyebrows.

"I think Ogden and Tom are fools," she said crisply. "They have good farms here. What do they want to go west for, or you, either? Don't get silly notions in your head, Wes."

Wesley flushed.

"Wouldn't you go with me, Dosia?" he said, trying to speak lightly.

"No, I wouldn't," said Theodosia, in her calm, sweet voice. Her face was serene, but the little wrinkle had grown deeper. Old Jim Parmelee would have known what it meant. He had seen the same expression on old Henry Ford's face many a time.

Wesley laughed good-humouredly, as if at a child. His heart was suddenly set on going west, and he was sure he could soon bring Theodosia around. He did not say anything more about it just then. Wesley thought he knew how to manage women.

When he broached the subject again, two days later, Theodosia told him plainly that it was no use. She would never consent to leave Heatherton and all her friends and go out to the prairies. The idea was just rank foolishness, and he would soon see that himself.

All this Theodosia said calmly and sweetly, without any trace of temper or irritation. Wesley still believed that he could persuade her and he tried perseveringly for a fortnight. By the end of that time he discovered that Theodosia was not a great-great-granddaughter of old Henry Ford for nothing.

Not that Theodosia ever got angry. Neither did she laugh at him. She met his arguments and pleadings seriously enough, but she never wavered.

"If you go to Manitoba, Wes, you'll go alone," she said. "I'll never go, so there is no use in any more talking."

Wesley was a descendant of old Henry Ford too. Theodosia's unexpected opposition roused all the latent stubbornness of his nature. He went over to Centreville oftener, and kept his blood at fever heat talking to Greene and Cary, who wanted him to go with them and spared no pains at inducement.

The matter was gossiped about in Heatherton, of course. People knew that Wesley Brooke had caught "the western fever," and wanted to sell out and go to Manitoba, while Theodosia was opposed to it. They thought Dosia would have to give in in the end, but said it was a pity Wes Brooke couldn't be contented to stay where he was well off.

Theodosia's family naturally sided with her and tried to dissuade Wesley. But he was mastered by that resentful irritation, roused in a man by opposition where he thinks he should be master, which will drive him into any cause.

One day he told Theodosia that he was going. She was working her butter in her little, snowy-clean dairy under the great willows by the well. Wesley was standing in the doorway, his stout, broad-shouldered figure filling up the sunlit space. He was frowning and sullen.

"I'm going west in two weeks' time with the boys, Dosia," he said stubbornly. "You can come with me or stay here—just exactly as you please. But I'm going."

Theodosia went on spatting her balls of golden butter on the print in silence. She was looking very neat and pretty in her big white apron, her sleeves rolled up high above her plump, dimpled elbows, and her ruddy hair curling about her face and her white throat. She looked as pliable as her butter.

Her silence angered her husband. He shuffled impatiently.

"Well, what have you to say, Dosia?"

"Nothing," said Theodosia. "If you have made up your mind to go, go you will, I suppose. But I will not. There is no use in talking. We've been over the ground often enough, Wes. The matter is settled."

Up to that moment Wesley had always believed that his wife would yield at last, when she saw that he was determined. Now he realized that she never would. Under that exterior of milky, dimpled flesh and calm blue eyes was all the iron will of old dead and forgotten Henry Ford. This mildest and meekest of girls and wives was not to be moved a hairsbreadth by all argument or entreaty, or insistence on a husband's rights.

A great, sudden anger came over the man. He lifted his hand and for one moment it seemed to Theodosia as if he meant to strike her. Then he dropped it with the first oath that had ever crossed his lips.

"You listen to me," he said thickly. "If you won't go with me I'll never come back here—never. When you want to do your duty as a wife you can come to me. But I'll never come back."

He turned on his heel and strode away. Theodosia kept on spatting her butter. The little perpendicular wrinkle had come between her brows again. At that moment an odd, almost uncanny resemblance to the old portrait of her great-great-grandfather, which hung on the parlour wall at home, came out on her girlish face.

The fortnight passed by. Wesley was silent and sullen, never speaking to his wife when he could avoid it. Theodosia was as sweet and serene as ever. She made an extra supply of shirts and socks for him, put up his lunch basket, and packed his trunk carefully. But she never spoke of his journey.

He did not sell his farm. Irving Brooke rented it. Theodosia was to live in the house. The business arrangements were simple and soon concluded.

Heatherton folks gossiped a great deal. They all condemned Theodosia. Even her own people sided against her now. They hated to be mixed up in a local scandal, and since Wes was bound to go they told Theodosia that it was her duty to go with him, no matter how much she disliked it. It would be disgraceful not to. They might as well have talked to the four winds. Theodosia was immoveable. They coaxed and argued and blamed—it all came to the same thing. Even those of them who could be "set" enough themselves on occasion could not understand Theodosia, who had always been so tractable. They finally gave up, as Wesley had done, baffled. Time would bring her to her senses, they said; you just had to leave that still, stubborn kind alone.

On the morning of Wesley's departure Theodosia arose at sunrise and prepared a tempting breakfast. Irving Brooke's oldest son, Stanley, who was to drive Wesley to the station, came over early with his express wagon. Wesley's trunk, corded and labelled, stood on the back platform. The breakfast was a very silent meal. When it was over Wesley put on his hat and overcoat and went to the door, around which Theodosia's morning-glory vines were beginning to twine. The sun was not yet above the trees and the long shadows lay on the dewy grass. The wet leaves were flickering on the old maples that grew along the fence between the yard and the clover field beyond. The skies were all pearly blue, cleanswept of clouds. From the little farmhouse the green meadows sloped down to the valley, where a blue haze wound in and out like a glistening ribbon.

Theodosia went out and stood looking inscrutably on, while Wesley and Irving hoisted the trunk into the wagon and tied it. Then Wesley came up the porch steps and looked at her.

"Dosia," he said a little huskily, "I said I wouldn't ask you to go again, but I will. Will you come with me yet?"

"No," said Theodosia gently.

He held out his hand. He did not offer to kiss her.

"Goodbye, Dosia."

"Goodbye, Wes."

There was no tremor of an eyelash with her. Wesley smiled bitterly and turned away. When the wagon reached the end of the little lane he turned and looked back for the last time. Through all the years that followed he carried with him the picture of his wife as he saw her then, standing amid the airy shadows and wavering golden lights of the morning, the wind blowing the skirt of her pale blue wrapper about her feet and ruffling the locks of her bright hair into a delicate golden cloud. Then the wagon disappeared around a curve in the road, and Theodosia turned and went back into her desolate home.

For a time there was a great buzz of gossip over the affair. People wondered over it. Old Jim Parmelee understood better than the others. When he met Theodosia he looked at her with a curious twinkle in his keen old eyes.

"Looks as if a man could bend her any way he'd a mind to, doesn't she?" he said. "Looks is deceiving. It'll come out in her face by and by—she's too young yet, but it's there. It does seem unnatteral to see a woman so stubborn— you'd kinder look for it more in a man."

Wesley wrote a brief letter to Theodosia when he reached his destination. He said he was well and was looking about for the best place to settle. He liked the country fine. He was at a place called Red Butte and guessed he'd locate there.

Two weeks later he wrote again. He had taken up a claim of three hundred acres. Greene and Cary had done the same. They were his nearest neighbours and were three miles away. He had knocked up a little shack, was learning to cook his own meals, and was very busy. He thought the country was a grand one and the prospects good.

Theodosia answered his letter and told him all the Heatherton news. She signed herself "Theodosia Brooke," but otherwise there was nothing in the letter to indicate that it was written by a wife to her husband.

At the end of a year Wesley wrote and once more asked her to go out to him. He was getting on well, and was sure she would like the place. It was a little rough, to be sure, but time would improve that.

"Won't you let bygones be bygones, Dosia?" he wrote, "and come out to me. Do, my dear wife."

Theodosia wrote back, refusing to go. She never got any reply, nor did she write again.

People had given up talking about the matter and asking Theodosia when she was going out to Wes. Heatherton had grown used to the chronic scandal within its decorous borders. Theodosia never spoke of her husband to anyone, and it was known that they did not correspond. She took her youngest sister to live with her. She had her garden and hens and a cow. The farm brought her enough to live on, and she was always busy.

When fifteen years had gone by there were naturally some changes in Heatherton, sleepy and; unprogressive as it was. Most of the old people were in the little hillside burying-ground that fronted the sunrise. Old Jim Parmelee was there with his recollections of four generations. Men and women who had been in their prime when Wesley went away were old now and the children were grown up and married.

Theodosia was thirty-five and was nothing like! the slim, dimpled girl who had stood on the porch steps and watched her husband drive away that morning fifteen years ago. She was stout and comely; the auburn hair was darker and arched away from her face in smooth, shining waves instead of the old-time curls. Her face was unlined and fresh-coloured, but no woman could live in subjection to her own unbending will for so many years and not show it. Nobody, looking at Theodosia now, would have found it hard to believe that a woman with such a determined, immoveable face could stick to a course of conduct in defiance of circumstances.

Wesley Brooke was almost forgotten. People knew, through correspondents of Greene and Cary, that he had prospered and grown rich. The curious old story had crystallized into accepted history.

A life may go on without ripple or disturbance for so many years that it may seem to have settled into a lasting calm; then a sudden wind of passion may sweep over it and leave behind a wake of tempestuous waters. Such a time came at last to Theodosia.

One day in August Mrs. Emory Merritt dropped in. Emory Merritt's sister was Ogden Greene's wife, and the Merritts kept up an occasional correspondence with her. Hence, Cecilia Merritt always knew what was to be known about Wesley Brooke, and always told Theodosia because she had never been expressly forbidden to do so.

Today she looked slightly excited. Secretly she was wondering if the news she brought would have any effect whatever on Theodosia's impassive calm.

"Do you know, Dosia, Wesley's real sick? In fact, Phoebe Greene says they have very poor hopes of him. He was kind of ailing all the spring, it seems, and about a month ago he was took down with some kind of slow fever they have out there. Phoebe says they have a hired nurse from the nearest town and a good doctor, but she reckons he won't get over it. That fever goes awful hard with a man of his years."

Cecilia Merritt, who was the fastest talker in Heatherton, had got this out before she was brought up by a queer sound, half gasp, half cry, from Theodosia. The latter looked as if someone had struck her a physical blow.

"Mercy, Dosia, you ain't going to faint! I didn't suppose you'd care. You never seemed to care."

"Did you say," asked Theodosia thickly, "that Wesley was sick—dying?"

"Well, that's what Phoebe said. She may be mistaken. Dosia Brooke, you're a queer woman. I never could make you out and I never expect to. I guess only the Lord who made you can translate you."

Theodosia stood up. The sun was getting low, and the valley beneath them, ripening to harvest, was like a river of gold. She folded up her sewing with a steady hand.

"It's five o'clock, so I'll ask you to excuse me, Cecilia. I have a good deal to attend to. You can ask Emory if he'll drive me to the station in the morning. I'm going out to Wes."

"Well, for the land's sake," said Cecilia Merritt feebly, as she tied on her gingham sunbonnet. She got up and went home in a daze.

Theodosia packed her trunk and worked all night, dry-eyed, with agony and fear tearing at her heart. The iron will had snapped at last, like a broken reed, and fierce self-condemnation seized on her. "I've been a wicked woman," she moaned.

A week from that day Theodosia climbed down from the dusty stage that had brought her from the station over the prairies to the unpretentious little house where Wesley Brooke lived. A young girl, so like what Ogden Greene's wife had been fifteen years before that Theodosia involuntarily exclaimed,

"Phoebe," came to the door. Beyond her, Theodosia saw the white-capped nurse.

Her voice trembled.

"Does—does Wesley Brooke live here?" she asked.

The girl nodded.

"Yes. But he is very ill at present. Nobody is allowed to see him."

Theodosia put up her hand and loosened her bonnet strings as if they were choking her. She had been sick with the fear that Wesley would be dead before she got to him. The relief was almost overwhelming.

"But I must see him," she cried hysterically—she, the calm, easy-going Dosia, hysterical—"I am his wife—and oh, if he had died before I got here!"

The nurse came forward.

"In that case I suppose you must," she conceded. "But he does not expect you. I must prepare him for the surprise."

She turned to the door of a room opening off the kitchen, but Theodosia, who had hardly heard her, was before her. She was inside the room before the nurse could prevent her. Then she stood, afraid and trembling, her eyes searching the dim apartment hungrily.

When they fell on the occupant of the bed Theodosia started in bitter surprise. All unconsciously she had been expecting to find Wesley as he had been when they parted. Could this gaunt, haggard creature, with the unkempt beard and prematurely grey hair and the hollow, beseeching eyes, be the ruddy, boyish-faced husband of her youth? She gave a choking cry of pain and shame, and the sick man turned his head. Their eyes met.

Amazement, incredulity, hope, dread, all flashed in succession over Wesley Brooke's lined face. He raised himself feebly up.

"Dosia," he murmured.

Theodosia staggered across the room and fell on her knees by the bed. She clasped his head to her breast and kissed him again and again.

"Oh, Wes, Wes, can you forgive me? I've been a wicked, stubborn woman—and I've spoiled our lives. Forgive me."

He held his thin trembling arms around her and devoured her face with his eyes.

"Dosia, when did you come? Did you know I was sick?"

"Wes, I can't talk till you say you've forgiven me."

"Oh, Dosia, you have just as much to forgive. We were both too set. I should have been more considerate."

"Just say, 'I forgive you, Dosia,'" she entreated.

"I forgive you, Dosia," he said gently, "and oh, it's so good to see you once more, darling. There hasn't been an hour since I left you that I haven't longed for your sweet face. If I had thought you really cared I'd have gone back. But I thought you didn't. It broke my heart. You did though, didn't you?"

"Oh, yes, yes, yes," she said, holding him more closely, with her tears falling.

When the young doctor from Red Butte came that evening he found a great improvement in his patient. Joy and happiness, those world-old physicians, had done what drugs and medicines had failed to do.

"I'm going to get better, Doc," said Wesley. "My wife has come and she's going to stay. You didn't know I was married, did you? I'll tell you the story some day. I proposed going back east, but Dosia says she'd rather stay here. I'm the happiest man in Red Butte, Doc."

He squeezed Theodosia's hand as he had used to do long ago in Heatherton church, and Dosia smiled down at him. There were no dimples now, but her smile was very sweet. The ghostly finger of old Henry Ford, pointing down through the generations, had lost its power to brand with its malediction the life of these, his descendants. Wesley and Theodosia had joined hands with their long-lost happiness.

The Story of an Invitation

Bertha Sutherland hurried home from the post office and climbed the stairs of her boarding-house to her room on the third floor. Her roommate, Grace Maxwell, was sitting on the divan by the window, looking out into the twilight.

A year ago Bertha and Grace had come to Dartmouth to attend the Academy, and found themselves roommates. Bertha was bright, pretty and popular, the favourite of her classmates and teachers; Grace was a grave, quiet girl, dressed in mourning. She was quite alone in the world, the aunt who had brought her up having recently died. At first she had felt shy with bright and brilliant Bertha; but they soon became friends, and the year that followed was a very pleasant one. It was almost ended now, for the terminal exams had begun, and in a week's time the school would close for the holidays.

"Have some chocolates, Grace," said Bertha gaily. "I got such good news in my letter tonight that I felt I must celebrate it fittingly. So I went into Carter's and invested all my spare cash in caramels. It's really fortunate the term is almost out, for I'm nearly bankrupt. I have just enough left to furnish a 'tuck-out' for commencement night, and no more."

"What is your good news, may I ask?" said Grace.

"You know I have an Aunt Margaret—commonly called Aunt Meg—out at Riversdale, don't you? There never was such a dear, sweet, jolly aunty in the world. I had a letter from her tonight. Listen, I'll read you what she says."

I want you to spend your holidays with me, my dear. Mary Fairweather and Louise Fyshe and Lily Dennis are coming, too. So there is just room for one more, and that one must be yourself. Come to Riversdale when school closes, and I'll feed you on strawberries and cream and pound cake and doughnuts and mince pies, and all the delicious, indigestible things that school girls love and careful mothers condemn. Mary and Lou and Lil are girls after your own heart, I know, and you shall all do just as you like, and we'll have picnics and parties and merry doings galore.

"There," said Bertha, looking up with a laugh. "Isn't that lovely?"

"How delightful it must be to have friends like that to love you and plan for you," said Grace wistfully. "I am sure you will have a pleasant vacation, Bertie. As for me, I am going into Clarkman's bookstore until school reopens. I saw Mr. Clarkman today and he agreed to take me."

Bertha looked surprised. She had not known what Grace's vacation plans were.

"I don't think you ought to do that, Grace," she said thoughtfully. "You are not strong, and you need a good rest. It will be awfully trying to work at Clarkman's all summer."

"There is nothing else for me to do," said Grace, trying to speak cheerfully. "You know I'm as poor as the proverbial church mouse, Bertie, and the simple truth is that I can't afford to pay my board all summer and get my winter outfit unless I do something to earn it. I shall be too busy to be lonesome, and I shall expect long, newsy letters from you, telling me all your fun—passing your vacation on to me at second-hand, you see. Well, I must set to work at those algebra problems. I tried them before dark, but I couldn't solve them. My head ached and I felt so stupid. How glad I shall be when exams are over."

"I suppose I must revise that senior English this evening," said Bertha absently.

But she made no move to do so. She was studying her friend's face. How very pale and thin Grace looked—surely much paler and thinner than when she had come to the Academy, and she had not by any means been plump and rosy then.

I believe she could not stand two months at Clarkman's, thought Bertha. If I were not going to Aunt Meg's, I would ask her to go home with me. Or even if Aunt Meg had room for another guest, I'd just write her all about Grace and ask if I could bring her with me. Aunt Meg would understand—she always understands. But she hasn't, so it can't be.

Just then a thought darted into Bertha's brain.

"What nonsense!" she said aloud so suddenly and forcibly that Grace fairly jumped.

"What is?"

"Oh, nothing much," said Bertha, getting up briskly. "See here, I'm going to get to work. I've wasted enough time."

She curled herself up on the divan and tried to study her senior English. But her thoughts wandered hopelessly, and finally she gave it up in despair and went to bed. There she could not sleep; she lay awake and wrestled with herself. It was after midnight when she sat up in bed and said solemnly, "I will do it."

Next day Bertha wrote a confidential letter to Aunt Meg. She thanked her for her invitation and then told her all about Grace.

"And what I want to ask, Aunt Meg, is that you will let me transfer my invitation to Grace, and ask her to go to Riversdale this summer in my place. Don't think me ungrateful. No, I'm sure you won't, you always understand things. But you can't have us both, and I'd rather Grace should go. It will do her so much good, and I have a lovely home of my own to go to, and she has none."

Aunt Meg understood, as usual, and was perfectly willing. So she wrote to Bertha and enclosed a note of invitation for Grace.

I shall have to manage this affair very carefully, reflected Bertha. Grace must never suspect that I did it on purpose. I will tell her that circumstances have prevented me from accepting Aunt Meg's invitation. That is true enough —no need to say that the circumstances are hers, not mine. And I'll say I just asked Aunt Meg to invite her in my place and that she has done so.

When Grace came home from her history examination that day, Bertha told her story and gave her Aunt Meg's cordial note.

"You must come to me in Bertha's place," wrote the latter. "I feel as if I knew you from her letters, and I will consider you as a sort of honorary niece, and I'll treat you as if you were Bertha herself."

"Isn't it splendid of Aunt Meg?" said Bertha diplomatically. "Of course you'll go, Gracie."

"Oh, I don't know," said Grace in bewilderment. "Are you sure you don't want to go, Bertha?"

"Indeed, I do want to go, dreadfully," said Bertha frankly. "But as I've told you, it is impossible. But if I am disappointed, Aunt Meg musn't be. You must go, Grace, and that is all there is about it."

In the end, Grace did go, a little puzzled and doubtful still, but thankful beyond words to escape the drudgery of the counter and the noise and heat of the city. Bertha went home, feeling a little bit blue in secret, it cannot be denied, but also feeling quite sure that if she had to do it all over again, she would do just the same.

The summer slipped quickly by, and finally two letters came to Bertha, one from Aunt Meg and one from Grace.

"I've had a lovely time," wrote the latter, "and, oh, Bertie, what do you think? I am to stay here always. Oh, of course I am going back to school next month, but this is to be my home after this. Aunt Meg—she makes me call her that—says I must stay with her for good."

In Aunt Meg's letter was this paragraph:

Grace is writing to you, and will have told you that I intend to keep her here. You know I have always wanted a daughter of my own, but my greedy brothers and sisters would never give me one of theirs. So I intend to adopt Grace. She is the sweetest girl in the world, and I am very grateful to you for sending her here. You will not know her when you see her. She has grown plump and rosy.

Bertha folded her letters up with a smile. "I have a vague, delightful feeling that I am the good angel in a storybook," she said.

The Touch of Fate

Mrs. Major Hill was in her element. This did not often happen, for in the remote prairie town of the Canadian Northwest, where her husband was stationed, there were few opportunities for match-making. And Mrs. Hill was —or believed herself to be—a born matchmaker.

Major Hill was in command of the detachment of Northwest Mounted Police at Dufferin Bluff. Mrs. Hill was wont to declare that it was the most forsaken place to be found in Canada or out of it; but she did her very best to brighten it up, and it is only fair to say that the N.W.M.P., officers and men, seconded her efforts.

When Violet Thayer came west to pay a long-promised visit to her old schoolfellow, Mrs. Hill's cup of happiness bubbled over. In her secret soul she vowed that Violet should never go back east unless it were post-haste to prepare a wedding trousseau. There were at least half a dozen eligibles among the M.P.s, and Mrs. Hill, after some reflection, settled on Ned Madison as the flower of the flock.

"He and Violet are simply made for each other," she told Major Hill the evening before Miss Thayer's arrival. "He has enough money and he is handsome and fascinating. And Violet is a beauty and a clever woman into the bargain. They can't help falling in love, I'm sure; it's fate!"

"Perhaps Miss Thayer may be booked elsewhere already," suggested Major Hill. He had seen more than one of his wife's card castles fall into heartbreaking ruin.

"Oh, no; Violet would have told me if that were the case. It's really quite time for her to think of settling down. She is twenty-five, you know. The men all go crazy over her, but she's dreadfully hard to please. However, she can't help liking Ned. He hasn't a single fault. I firmly believe it is foreordained."

And in this belief Mrs. Hill rested securely, but nevertheless did not fail to concoct several feminine artifices for the helping on of foreordination. It was a working belief with her that it was always well to have the gods in your debt.

Violet Thayer came, saw, and conquered. Within thirty-six hours of her arrival at Dufferin Bluff she had every one of the half-dozen eligibles at her feet, not to mention a score or more ineligibles. She would have been surprised indeed had it been otherwise. Miss Thayer knew her power, and was somewhat unduly fond of exercising it. But she was a very nice girl into the bargain, and so thought one and all of the young men who frequented Mrs. Hill's drawing-room and counted it richly worth while merely to look at Miss Thayer after having seen nothing for weeks except flabby half-breed girls and blue-haired squaws.

Madison was foremost in the field, of course. Madison was really a nice fellow, and quite deserved all Mrs. Hill's encomiums. He was good-looking and well groomed—could sing and dance divinely and play the violin to perfection. The other M.P.s were all jealous of him, and more so than ever when Violet Thayer came. They did not consider that any one of them had the ghost of a chance if Madison entered the lists against them.

Violet liked Madison, and was very chummy with him after her own fashion. She thought all the M.P.s were nice boys, and they amused her, for which she was grateful. She had expected Dufferin Bluff to be very dull, and doubtless it would pall after a time, but for a change it was delightful.

The sixth evening after her arrival found Mrs. Hill's room crowded, as usual, with M.P.s. Violet was looking her best in a distracting new gown—Sergeant Fox afterwards described it to a brother officer as a "stunning sort of rig between a cream and a blue and a brown"; she flirted impartially with all the members of her circle at first, but gradually narrowed down to Ned Madison, much to the delight of Mrs. Hill, who was hovering around like a small, brilliant butterfly.

Violet was talking to Madison and watching John Spencer out of the tail of her eye. Spencer was not an M.P. He had some government post at Dufferin Bluff, and this was his first call at Lone Poplar Villa since Miss Thayer's arrival. He did not seem to be dazzled by her at all, and after his introduction had promptly retired to a corner with Major Hill, where they talked the whole evening about the trouble on the Indian reservation at Loon Lake.

Possibly this indifference piqued Miss Thayer. Possibly she considered it refreshing after the servile adulation of the M.P.s. At any rate, when all the latter were gathered about the piano singing a chorus with gusto, she shook Madison off and went over to the corner where Spencer, deserted by the Major, whose bass was wanted, was sitting in solitary state.

He looked up indifferently as Violet shimmered down on the divan beside him. Sergeant Robinson, who was watching them jealously from the corner beyond the palms, and would have given his eyes, or at least one of them, for such a favour, mentally vowed that Spencer was the dullest fellow he had ever put those useful members on.

"Don't you sing, Mr. Spencer?" asked Violet by way of beginning a conversation, as she turned her splendid eyes full upon him. Robinson would have lost his head under them, but Spencer kept his heroically.

"No," was his calmly brief reply, given without any bluntness, but with no evident intention of saying anything more.

In spite of her social experience Violet felt disconcerted.

"If he doesn't want to talk to me I won't try to make him," she thought crossly. No man had ever snubbed her so before.

Spencer listened immovably to the music for a time. Then he turned to his companion with a palpable effort to be civilly sociable.

"How do you like the west, Miss Thayer?" he said.

Violet smiled—the smile most men found dangerous.

"Very much, so far as I have seen it. There is a flavour about the life here that I like, but I dare say it would soon pall. It must be horribly lonesome here most of the time, especially in winter."

"The M.P.s are always growling that it is," returned Spencer with a slight smile. "For my own part I never find it so."

Violet decided that his smile was very becoming to him and that she liked the way his dark hair grew over his forehead.

"I don't think I've seen you at Lone Poplar Villa before?" she said.

"No. I haven't been here for some time. I came up tonight to see the Major about the Loon Lake trouble."

"Otherwise you wouldn't have come," thought Violet. "Flattering—very!" Aloud she said, "Is it serious?"

"Oh, no. A mere squabble among the Indians. Have you ever visited the Reservation, Miss Thayer? No? Well, you should get some of your M.P. friends to take you out. It would be worth while."

"Why don't you ask me to go yourself?" said Violet audaciously.

Spencer smiled again. "Have I failed in politeness by not doing so? I fear you would find me an insufferably dull companion."

So he was not going to ask her after all. Violet felt piqued. She was also conscious of a sensation very near akin to disappointment. She looked across at Madison. How trim and dapper he was!

"I hate a bandbox man," she said to herself.

Spencer meanwhile had picked up one of Mrs. Hill's novels from the stand beside him.

"Fools of Habit," he said, glancing at the cover. "I see it is making quite a sensation down east. I suppose you've read it?"

"Yes. It is very frivolous and clever—all froth but delightful froth. Did you like it?"

Spencer balanced the novel reflectively on his slender brown hand.

"Well, yes, rather. But I don't care for novels as a rule. I don't understand them. The hero of this book, now—do you believe that a man in love would act as he did?"

"I don't know," said Violet amusedly. "You ought to be a better judge than I. You are a man."

"I have never loved anybody, so I am in no position to decide," said Spencer.

There was as little self-consciousness in his voice as if he were telling her a fact concerning the Loon Lake trouble. Violet rose to the occasion.

"You have an interesting experience to look forward to," she said.

Spencer turned his deep-set grey eyes squarely upon her.

"I don't know that. When I said I had never loved, I meant more than the love of a man for some particular woman. I meant love in every sense. I do not know what it is to have an affection for any human being. My parents died before I can remember. My only living relative was a penurious old uncle who brought me up for shame's sake and kicked me out on the world as soon as he could. I don't make friends easily. I have a few acquaintances whom I like, but there is not a soul on earth for whom I care, or who cares for me."

"What a revelation love will be to you when it comes," said Violet softly. Again he looked into her eyes.

"Do you think it will come?" he asked.

Before she could reply Mrs. Hill pounced upon them. Violet was wanted to sing. Mr. Spencer would excuse her, wouldn't he? Mr. Spencer did so obligingly. Moreover, he got up and bade his hostess good night. Violet gave him her hand.

"You will call again?" she said.

Spencer looked across at Madison—perhaps it was accidental.

"I think not," he said. "If, as you say, love will come some time, it would be a very unpleasant revelation if it came in hopeless guise, and one never knows what may happen."

Miss Thayer was conscious of a distinct fluttering of her heart as she went across to the piano. This was a new sensation for her, and worthy of being analyzed. After the M.P.s had gone she asked Mrs. Hill who Mr. Spencer was.

"Oh, John Spencer," said Mrs. Hill carelessly. "He's at the head of the Land Office here. That's really all I know about him. Jack says he is a downright good fellow and all that, you know. But he's no earthly good in a social way; he can't talk or he won't. He's flat. So different from Mr. Madison, isn't he?"

"Very," said Violet emphatically.

After Mrs. Hill had gone out Violet walked to the nearest mirror and looked at herself with her forefinger in the dimple of her chin.

"It is very odd," she said. She did not mean the dimple.

Spencer had told her he was not coming back. She did not believe this, but she did not expect him for a few days. Consequently, when he appeared the very next evening she was surprised. Madison, to whom she was talking when Spencer entered, does not know to this day what she had started to say to him, for she never finished her sentence.

"I wonder if it is the Loon Lake affair again?" she thought nervously.

Mrs. Hill came up at this point and whisked Madison off for a waltz. Spencer, seeing his chance, came straight across the room to her. Sergeant Robinson, who was watching them as usual, is willing to make affidavit that Miss Thayer changed colour.

After his greeting Spencer said nothing. He sat beside her, and they watched Mrs. Hill and Madison dancing. Violet wondered why she did not feel bored. When she saw Madison coming back to her she was conscious of an unreasonable anger with him. She got up abruptly.

"Let us go out on the verandah," she said imperiously. "It is absolutely stifling in here."

They went out. It was very cool and dusky. The lights of the town twinkled out below them, and the prairie bluffs behind them were dark and sibilant.

"I am going to drive over to Loon Lake tomorrow afternoon to look into affairs there," said Spencer. "Will you go with me?"

Violet reflected a moment. "You didn't ask me as if you really wanted me to go," she said.

Spencer put his hand over the white fingers that rested on the railing. He bent forward until his breath stirred the tendrils of hair on her forehead.

"Yes, I do," he said distinctly. "I want you to go with me to Loon Lake tomorrow more than I ever wanted any thing in my life before."

Later on, when everybody had gone, Violet had her bad quarter of an hour with Mrs. Hill. That lady felt herself aggrieved.

"I think you treated poor Ned very badly tonight, Vi. He felt really blue over it. And it was awfully bad form to go out with Spencer as you did and stay there so long. And you oughtn't to flirt with him—he doesn't understand the game."

"I'm not going to flirt with him," said Miss Thayer calmly.

"Oh, I suppose it's just your way. Only don't turn the poor fellow's head.

By the way, Ned is coming up with his camera tomorrow afternoon to take us all."

"I'm afraid he won't find me at home," said Violet sweetly. "I am going out to Loon Lake with Mr. Spencer."

Mrs. Hill flounced off to bed in a pet. She was disgusted with everything, she declared to the Major. Things had been going so nicely, and now they were all muddled.

"Isn't Madison coming up to time?" queried the Major sleepily.

"Madison! It's Violet. She is behaving abominably. She treated poor Ned shamefully tonight. You saw yourself how she acted with Spencer, and she's going to Loon Lake with him tomorrow, she says. I'm sure I don't know what she can see in him. He's the dullest, pokiest fellow alive—so different from her in every way."

"Perhaps that is why she likes him," suggested the Major. "The attraction of opposites and all that, you know."

But Mrs. Hill crossly told him he didn't know anything about it, so, being a wise man, he held his tongue.

During the next two weeks Mrs. Hill was the most dissatisfied woman in the four districts, and every M.P. down to the rawest recruit anathemized Spencer in secret a dozen times a day. Violet simply dropped everyone else, including Madison, in the coolest, most unmistakable way.

One night Spencer did not come to Lone Poplar Villa. Violet looked for him to the last. When she realized that he was not coming she went to the verandah to have it out with herself. As she sat huddled up in a dim corner beneath a silkily rustling western maple two M.P.s came out and, not seeing her, went on with their conversation.

"Heard about Spencer?" questioned one.

"No. What of him?"

"Well, they say Miss Thayer's thrown him over. Yesterday I was passing here about four in the afternoon and I saw Spencer coming in. I went down to the Land Office and was chatting to Cribson when the door opened about half an hour later and Spencer burst in. He was pale as the dead, and looked wild. 'Has Fyshe gone to Rainy River about those Crown Lands yet?' he jerked out. Cribson said, 'No.' Then tell him he needn't; I'm going myself,' said Spencer and out he bolted. He posted off to Rainy River today, and won't be back for a fortnight. She'll be gone then."

"Rather rough on Spencer after the way she encouraged him," returned the other as they passed out of earshot.

Violet got up. All the callers were gone, and she swept in to Mrs. Hill dramatically.

"Edith," she said in the cold, steady voice that, to those who knew her, meant breakers ahead for somebody, "Mr. Spencer was here yesterday when I was riding with the Major, was he not? What did you tell him about me?"

Mrs. Hill looked at Violet's blazing eyes and wilted.

"I—didn't tell him anything—much."

"What was it?"

Mrs. Hill began to sob.

"Don't look at me like that, Violet! He just dropped in and we were talking about you—at least I was—and I had heard that Harry St. Maur was paying you marked attention before you came west—and—and that some people thought you were engaged—and so—and so—"

"You told Mr. Spencer that I was engaged to Harry St. Maur?"

"No-o-o—I just hinted. I didn't mean an-any harm. I never dreamed you'd really c-care. I thought you were just amusing yourself—and so did everybody —and I wanted Ned Madison—"

Violet had turned very pale.

"I love him," she said hoarsely, "and you've sent him away. He's gone to Rainy River. I shall never see him again!"

"Oh, yes, you will," gasped Mrs. Hill faintly. "He'll come back when he knows—you c-can write and tell him—"

"Do you suppose I am going to write and ask him to come back?" said Violet wildly. "I've enough pride left yet to keep me from doing that for a man at whose head I've thrown myself openly—yes, openly, and who has never, in words at least, told me he cared anything about me. I will never forgive you, Edith!"

Then Mrs. Hill found herself alone with her lacerated feelings. After soothing them with a good cry, she set to work thinking seriously. There was no doubt she had muddled things badly, but there was no use leaving them in a muddle when a word or two fitly spoken might set them straight.

Mrs. Hill sat down and wrote a very diplomatic letter before she went to bed, and the next morning she waylaid Sergeant Fox and asked him if he would ride down to Rainy River with a very important message for Mr. Spencer. Sergeant Fox wondered what it could be, but it was not his to reason why; it was his only to mount and ride with all due speed, for Mrs. Hill's whims and wishes were as stringent and binding as the rules of the force.

That evening when Mrs. Hill and Violet—the latter very silent and regal—were sitting on the verandah, a horseman came galloping up the Rainy River trail. Mrs. Hill excused herself and went in. Five minutes later John Spencer, covered with the alkali dust of his twenty miles' ride, dismounted at Violet's side.

The M.P.s gave a concert at the barracks that night and Mrs. Hill and her Major went to it, as well as everyone else of any importance in town except Violet and Spencer. They sat on Major Hill's verandah and watched the moon rising over the bluffs and making milk-white reflections in the prairie lakes.

"It seems a year of misery since last night," sighed Violet happily.

"You couldn't have been quite as miserable as I was," said Spencer earnestly. "You were everything—absolutely everything to me. Other men have little rills and driblets of affection for sisters and cousins and aunts, but everything in me went out to you. Do you remember you told me the first time we met that love would be a revelation to me? It has been more. It has been a new gospel. I hardly dared hope you could care for me. Even yet I don't know why you do."

"I love you," said Violet gravely, "because you are you."

Than which, of course, there could be no better reason.

The Waking of Helen

Robert Reeves looked somewhat curiously at the girl who was waiting on him at his solitary breakfast. He had not seen her before, arriving at his summer boarding house only the preceding night.

It was a shabby farmhouse on the inland shore of a large bay that was noted for its tides, and had wonderful possibilities of light and shade for an impressionist. Reeves was an enthusiastic artist. It mattered little to him that the boarding accommodations were most primitive, the people uncultured and dull, the place itself utterly isolated, as long as he could revel in those transcendent sunsets and sunrises, those marvellous moonlights, those wonderful purple shores and sweeps of shimmering blue water.

The owner of the farm was Angus Fraser, and he and his wife seemed to be a reserved, uncouth pair, with no apparent interest in life save to scratch a bare living out of their few stony acres. He had an impression that they were childless and was at a loss to place this girl who poured his tea and brought in his toast. She did not resemble either Fraser or his wife. She was certainly not beautiful, being very tall and rather awkward, and dressed in a particularly unbecoming dark print wrapper. Her luxuriant hair was thick and black, and was coiled in a heavy knot at the nape of her neck. Her features were delicate but irregular, and her skin was very brown. Her eyes attracted Reeves's notice especially; they were large and dark and full of a half-unconscious, wistful longing, as if a prisoned soul behind them were vainly trying to reveal itself.

Reeves could find out nothing of her from herself, for she responded to his tentative questions about the place in the briefest fashion. Afterwards he interviewed Mrs. Fraser cautiously, and ascertained that the girl's name was Helen Fraser, and that she was Angus's niece.

"Her father and mother are dead and we've brought her up. Helen's a good girl in most ways—a little obstinate and sulky now and then—but generally she's steady enough, and as for work, there ain't a girl in Bay Beach can come up to her in house or field. Angus calculates she saves him a man's wages clear. No, I ain't got nothing to say against Helen."

Nevertheless, Reeves felt somehow that Mrs. Fraser did not like her husband's niece. He often heard her scolding or nagging Helen at her work, and noticed that the latter never answered back. But once, after Mrs. Angus's tongue had been especially bitter, he met the girl hurrying along the hall from the kitchen with her eyes full of tears. Reeves felt as if someone had struck him a blow. He went to Angus and his wife that afternoon. He wished to paint a shore picture, he said, and wanted a model. Would they allow Miss Fraser to pose for him? He would pay liberally for her time.

Angus and his wife had no objection. They would pocket the money, and Helen could be spared a spell every day as well as not. Reeves told Helen of his plan himself, meeting her in the evening as she was bringing the cows home from the low shore pastures beyond the marsh. He was surprised at the sudden illumination of her face. It almost transfigured her from a plain, sulky-looking girl into a beautiful woman.

But the glow passed quickly. She assented to his plan quietly, almost lifelessly. He walked home with her behind the cows and talked of the sunset and the mysterious beauty of the bay and the purple splendour of the distant coasts. She listened in silence. Only once, when he spoke of the distant murmur of the open sea, she lifted her head and looked at him.

"What does it say to you?" she asked.

"It speaks of eternity. And to you?"

"It calls me," she answered simply, "and then I want to go out and meet it

—and it hurts me too. I can't tell how or why. Sometimes it makes me feel as if I were asleep and wanted to wake and didn't know how."

She turned and looked out over the bay. A dying gleam of sunset broke through a cloud and fell across her hair. For a moment she seemed the spirit of the shore personified—all its mystery, all its uncertainty, all its elusive charm.

She has possibilities, thought Reeves.

Next day he began his picture. At first he had thought of painting her as the incarnation of a sea spirit, but decided that her moods were too fitful. So he began to sketch her as "Waiting"—a woman looking out across the bay with a world of hopeless longing in her eyes. The subject suited her well, and the picture grew apace.

When he was tired of work he made her walk around the shore with him, or row up the head of the bay in her own boat. He tried to draw her out, at first with indifferent success. She seemed to be frightened of him. He talked to her of many things—the far outer world whose echoes never reached her, foreign lands where he had travelled, famous men and women whom he had met, music, art and books. When he spoke of books he touched the right chord. One of those transfiguring flashes he delighted to evoke now passed over her plain face.

"That is what I've always wanted," she said hungrily, "and I never get them. Aunt hates to see me reading. She says it is a waste of time. And I love it so. I read every scrap of paper I can get hold of, but I hardly ever see a book."

The next day Reeves took his Tennyson to the shore and began to read the Idylls of the King to her.

"It is beautiful," was her sole verbal comment, but her rapt eyes said everything.

After that he never went out with her without a book—now one of the poets, now some prose classic. He was surprised by her quick appreciation of and sympathy with the finest passages. Gradually, too, she forgot her shyness and began to talk. She knew nothing of his world, but her own world she knew and knew well. She was a mine of traditional history about the bay. She knew the rocky coast by heart, and every old legend that clung to it. They drifted into making excursions along the shore and explored its wildest retreats. The girl had an artist's eye for scenery and colour effect.

"You should have been an artist," Reeves told her one day when she had pointed out to him the exquisite loveliness of a shaft of light falling through a cleft in the rocks across a dark-green pool at their base.

"I would rather be a writer," she said slowly, "if I could only write something like those books you have read to me. What a glorious destiny it must be to have something to say that the whole world is listening for, and to be able to say it in words that will live forever! It must be the noblest human lot."

"Yet some of those men and women were neither good nor noble," said Reeves gently, "and many of them were unhappy."

Helen dismissed the subject as abruptly as she always did when the conversation touched too nearly on the sensitive edge of her soul dreams.

"Do you know where I am taking you today?" she said.

"No—where?"

"To what the people here call the Kelpy's Cave. I hate to go there. I believe there is something uncanny about it, but I think you will like to see it. It is a dark little cave in the curve of a small cove, and on each side the headlands of rock run far out. At low tide we can walk right around, but when the tide comes in it fills the Kelpy's Cave. If you were there and let the tide come past the points, you would be drowned unless you could swim, for the rocks are so steep and high it is impossible to climb them."

Reeves was interested.

"Was anyone ever caught by the tide?"

"Yes," returned Helen, with a shudder. "Once, long ago, before I was born, a girl went around the shore to the cave and fell asleep there—and the tide came in and she was drowned. She was young and very pretty, and was to have been married the next week. I've been afraid of the place ever since."

The treacherous cave proved to be a picturesque and innocent-looking spot, with the beach of glittering sand before it and the high gloomy walls of rock on either hand.

"I must come here some day and sketch it," said Reeves enthusiastically, "and you must be the Kelpy, Helen, and sit in the cave with your hair wrapped about you and seaweed clinging to it."

"Do you think a kelpy would look like that?" said the girl dreamily. "I don't. I think it is a wild, wicked little sea imp, malicious and mocking and cruel, and it sits here and watches for victims."

"Well, never mind your sea kelpies," Reeves said, fishing out his Longfellow. "They are a tricky folk, if all tales be true, and it is supposed to be a very rash thing to talk about them in their own haunts. I want to read you 'The Building of the Ship.' You will like it, I'm sure."

When the tide turned they went home.

"We haven't seen the kelpy, after all," said Reeves.

"I think I shall see him some day," said Helen gravely. "I think he is waiting for me there in that gloomy cave of his, and some time or other he will get me."

Reeves smiled at the gloomy fancy, and Helen smiled back at him with one of her sudden radiances. The tide was creeping swiftly up over the white sands. The sun was low and the bay was swimming in a pale blue glory. They parted at Clam Point, Helen to go for the cows and Reeves to wander on up the shore. He thought of Helen at first, and the wonderful change that had come over her of late; then he began to think of another face—a marvellously lovely one with blue eyes as tender as the waters before him. Then Helen was forgotten.

The summer waned swiftly. One afternoon Reeves took a fancy to revisit the Kelpy's Cave. Helen could not go. It was harvest time, and she was needed in the field.

"Don't let the kelpy catch you," she said to him half seriously. "The tide will turn early this afternoon, and you are given to day-dreaming."

"I'll be careful," he promised laughingly, and he meant to be careful. But somehow when he reached the cave its unwholesome charm overcame him, and he sat down on the boulder at its mouth.

"An hour yet before tide time," he said. "Just enough time to read that article on impressionists in my review and then stroll home by the sandshore."

From reading he passed to day-dreaming, and day-dreaming drifted into sleep, with his head pillowed on the rocky walls of the cave.

How long he had slept he did not know, but he woke with a start of horror. He sprang to his feet, realizing his position instantly. The tide was in—far in past the headlands already. Above and beyond him towered the pitiless unscalable rocks. There was no way of escape.

Reeves was no coward, but life was sweet to him, and to die like that—like a drowned rat in a hole—to be able to do nothing but wait for that swift and sure oncoming death! He reeled against the damp rock wall, and for a moment sea and sky and prisoning headlands and white-lined tide whirled before his eyes.

Then his head grew clearer. He tried to think. How long had he? Not more than twenty minutes at the outside. Well, death was sure and he would meet it bravely. But to wait—to wait helplessly! He should go; mad with the horror of it before those endless minutes would have passed!

He took something from his pocket and bent his, head over it, pressing his lips to it repeatedly. And then, when he raised his face again, a dory was coming around the headland on his right, and Helen Fraser was in it.

Reeves was dizzy again with the shock of joy and thankfulness. He ran down over the little stretch of sand still uncovered by the tide and around to the rocks of the headlands against which the dory was already grating. He sprang forward impulsively and caught the girl's cold hands in his as she dropped the oars and stood up.

"Helen, you have saved me! How can I ever thank you? I—"

He broke off abruptly, for she was looking up at him, breathlessly and voicelessly, with her whole soul in her eyes. He saw in them a revelation that amazed him; he dropped her hands and stepped back as if she had struck him in the face.

Helen did not notice the change in him. She clasped her hands together and her voice trembled.

"Oh, I was afraid I should be too late! When I came in from the field Aunt Hannah said you had not come back—and I knew it was tide time—and I felt somehow that it had caught you in the cave. I ran down over the marsh and took Joe Simmon's dory. If I had not got here in time—"

She broke off shiveringly. Reeves stepped into the dory and took up the oars.

"The kelpy would have been sure of its victim then," he said, trying to speak lightly. "It would have almost served me right for neglecting your warning. I was very careless. You must let me row back. I am afraid you have overtasked your strength trying to cheat the kelpy."

Reeves rowed homeward in an absolute silence. Helen did not speak and he could not. When they reached the dory anchorage he helped her out.

"I think I'll go out to the Point for a walk," he said. "I want to steady my nerves. You must go right home and rest. Don't be anxious—I won't take any more chances with sea kelpies."

Helen went away without a word, and Reeves walked slowly out to the Point. He was grieved beyond measure at the discovery he believed he had made. He had never dreamed of such a thing. He was not a vain man, and was utterly free from all tendency to flirtation. It had never occurred to him that the waking of the girl's deep nature might be attended with disastrous consequences. He had honestly meant to help her, and what had he done?

He felt very uncomfortable; he could not conscientiously blame himself, but he saw that he had acted foolishly. And of course he must go away at once.

And he must also tell her something she ought to know. He wished he had told her long ago.

The following afternoon was a perfect one. Reeves was sketching on the sandshore when Helen came. She sat down on a camp stool a little to one side and did not speak. After a few moments Reeves pushed away his paraphernalia impatiently.

"I don't feel in a mood for work," he said. "It is too dreamy a day—one ought to do nothing to be in keeping. Besides, I'm getting lazy now that my vacation is nearly over. I must go in a few days."

He avoided looking at her, so he did not see the sudden pallor of her face.

"So soon?" she said in a voice expressive of no particular feeling.

"Yes. I ought not to have lingered so long. My world will be forgetting me and that will not do. It has been a very pleasant summer and I shall be sorry to leave Bay Beach."

"But you will come back next summer?" asked Helen quickly. "You said you would."

Reeves nerved himself for his very distasteful task.

"Perhaps," he said, with an attempt at carelessness, "but if I do so, I shall not come alone. Somebody who is very dear to me will come with me—as my wife. I have never told you about her, Helen, but you and I are such good friends that I do not mind doing so now. I am engaged to a very sweet girl, and we expect to be married next spring."

There was a brief silence. Reeves had been vaguely afraid of a scene and was immensely relieved to find his fear unrealized. Helen sat very still. He could not see her face. Did she care, after all? Was he mistaken?

When she spoke her voice was perfectly calm.

"Thank you, it is very kind of you to tell me about her. I suppose she is very beautiful."

"Yes, here is her picture. You can judge for yourself."

Helen took the portrait from his hand and looked at it steadily. It was a miniature painted on ivory, and the face looking out from it was certainly lovely.

"It is no wonder you love her," said the girl in a low tone as she handed it back. "It must be strange to be so beautiful as that."

Reeves picked up his Tennyson.

"Shall I read you something? What will you have?"

"Read 'Elaine,' please. I want to hear that once more."

Reeves felt a sudden dislike to her choice.

"Wouldn't you prefer something else?" he asked, hurriedly turning over the leaves. "'Elaine' is rather sad. Shan't I read 'Guinevere' instead?"

"No," said Helen in the same lifeless tone. "I have no sympathy for Guinevere. She suffered and her love was unlawful, but she was loved in return—she did not waste her love on someone who did not want or care for it. Elaine did, and her life went with it. Read me the story."

Reeves obeyed. When he had finished he held the book out to her.

"Helen, will you take this Tennyson from me in remembrance of our friendship and of the Kelpy's Cave? I shall never forget that I owe my life to you."

"Thank you."

She took the book and placed a little thread of crimson seaweed that had been caught in the sand between the pages of "Elaine." Then she rose.

"I must go back now. Aunt will need me. Thank you again for the book, Mr. Reeves, and for all your kindness to me."

Reeves was relieved when the interview was over. Her calmness had reassured him. She did not care very much, after all; it was only a passing fancy, and when he was gone she would soon forget him.

He went away a few days later, and Helen bade him an impassive good-bye. When the afternoon was far spent she stole away from the house to the shore, with her Tennyson in her hand, and took her way to the Kelpy's Cave.

The tide was just beginning to come in. She sat down on the big boulder where Reeves had fallen asleep. Beyond stretched the gleaming blue waters, mellowing into a hundred fairy shades horizonward.

The shadows of the rocks were around her. In front was the white line of the incoming tide; it had almost reached the headlands. A few minutes more and escape would be cut off—yet she did not move.

When the dark green water reached her, and the lapping wavelets swished up over the hem of her dress, she lifted her head and a sudden strange smile flashed over her face.

Perhaps the kelpy understood it.

The Way of the Winning of Anne

Jerome Irving had been courting Anne Stockard for fifteen years. He had begun when she was twenty and he was twenty-five, and now that Jerome was forty, and Anne, in a village where everybody knew everybody else's age, had to own to being thirty-five, the courtship did not seem any nearer a climax than it had at the beginning. But that was not Jerome's fault, poor fellow!

At the end of the first year he had asked Anne to marry him, and Anne had refused. Jerome was disappointed, but he kept his head and went on courting Anne just the same; that is he went over to Esek Stockard's house every Saturday night and spent the evening, he walked home with Anne from prayer meeting and singing school and parties when she would let him, and asked her to go to all the concerts and socials and quilting frolics that came off. Anne never would go, of course, but Jerome faithfully gave her the chance. Old Esek rather favoured Jerome's suit, for Anne was the plainest of his many daughters, and no other fellow seemed at all anxious to run Jerome off the track; but she took her own way with true Stockard firmness, and matters were allowed to drift on at the will of time or chance.

Three years later Jerome tried his luck again, with precisely the same result, and after that he had asked Anne regularly once a year to marry him, and just as regularly Anne said no a little more brusquely and a little more decidedly every year. Now, in the mellowness of a fifteen-year-old courtship, Jerome did not mind it at all. He knew that everything comes to the man who has patience to wait.

Time, of course, had not stood still with Anne and Jerome, or with the history of Deep Meadows. At the Stockard homestead the changes had been many and marked. Every year or two there had been a wedding in the big brick farmhouse, and one of old Esek's girls had been the bride each time. Julia and Grace and Celia and Betty and Theodosia and Clementina Stockard were all married and gone. But Anne had never had another lover. There had to be an old maid in every big family she said, and she was not going to marry Jerome Irving just for the sake of having Mrs. on her tombstone.

Old Esek and his wife had been put away in the Deep Meadows burying-ground. The broad, fertile Stockard acres passed into Anne's possession. She was a good business-woman, and the farm continued to be the best in the district. She kept two hired men and a servant girl, and the sixteen-year-old of her oldest sister lived with her. There were few visitors at the Stockard place now, but Jerome "dropped in" every Saturday night with clockwork regularity and talked to Anne about her stock and advised her regarding the rotation of her crops and the setting out of her orchards. And at ten o'clock he would take his hat and cane and tell Anne to be good to herself, and go home.

Anne had long since given up trying to discourage him; she even accepted attentions from him now that she had used to refuse. He always walked home with her from evening meetings and was her partner in the games at quilting parties. It was great fun for the young folks. "Old Jerome and Anne" were a standing joke in Deep Meadows. But the older people had ceased to expect anything to come of it.

Anne laughed at Jerome as she had always done, and would not have owned for the world that she could have missed him. Jerome was useful, she admitted, and a comfortable friend; and she would have liked him well enough if he would only omit that ridiculous yearly ceremony of proposal.

It was Jerome's fortieth birthday when Anne refused him again. He realized this as he went down the road in the moonlight, and doubt and dismay began to creep into his heart. Anne and he were both getting old—there was no disputing that fact. It was high time that he brought her to terms if he was ever going to. Jerome was an easy-going mortal and always took things placidly, but he did not mean to have all those fifteen years of patient courting go for nothing He had thought Anne would get tired of saying no, sooner or later, and say yes, if for no other reason than to have a change; but getting tired did not seem to run in the Stockard blood. She had said no that night just as coolly and decidedly and unsentimentally as she said it fifteen years before. Jerome had the sensation of going around in a circle and never getting any further on. He made up his mind that something must be done, and just as he got to the brook that divides Deep Meadows West from Deep Meadows Central an idea struck him; it was a good idea and amused him. He laughed aloud and slapped his thigh, much to the amusement of two boys who were sitting unnoticed on the railing of the bridge.

"There's old Jerome going home from seeing Anne Stockard," said one. "Wonder what on earth he's laughing at. Seems to me if I couldn't get a wife without hoeing a fifteen-year row, I'd give up trying."

But, then, the speaker was a Hamilton, and the Hamiltons never had any perseverance.

Jerome, although a well-to-do man, owning a good farm, had, so to speak, no home of his own. The old Irving homestead belonged to his older brother, who had a wife and family. Jerome lived with them and was so used to it he didn't mind.

At forty a lover must not waste time. Jerome thought out the details that night, and next day he opened the campaign. But it was not until the evening after that that Anne Stockard heard the news. It was her niece, Octavia, who told her. The latter had been having a chat up the lane with Sam Mitchell, and came in with a broad smile on her round, rosy face and a twinkle in her eyes.

"I guess you've lost your beau this time, Aunt Anne. It looks as if he meant to take you at your word at last."

"What on earth do you mean?" asked Anne, a little sharply. She was in the pantry counting eggs, and Octavia's interruption made her lose her count. "Now I can't remember whether it was six or seven dozen I said last. I shall have to count them all over again. I wish, Octavia, that you could think of something besides beaus all the time."

"Well, but listen," persisted Octavia wickedly. "Jerome Irving was at the social at the Cherry Valley parsonage last night, and he had Harriet Warren there—took her there, and drove her home again."

"I don't believe it," cried Anne, before she thought. She dropped an egg into the basket so abruptly that the shell broke.

"Oh, it's true enough. Sam Mitchell told me; he was there and saw him. Sam says he looked quite beaming, and was dressed to kill, and followed Harriet around like her shadow. I guess you won't have any more bother with him, Aunt Anne."

In the process of picking the broken egg out of the whole ones Anne had recovered her equanimity. She gave a careful little laugh.

"Well, it's to be hoped so. Goodness knows it's time he tried somebody else. Go and change your dress for milking, Octavia, and don't spend quite so much time gossiping up the lane with Sam Mitchell. He always was a fetch-and-carry. Young girls oughtn't to be so pert."

When the subdued Octavia had gone, Anne tossed the broken eggshell out of the pantry window viciously enough.

"There's no fool like an old fool. Jerome Irving always was an idiot. The idea of his going after Harriet Warren! He's old enough to be her father. And a Warren, too! I've seen the time an Irving wouldn't be seen on the same side of the road with a Warren. Well, anyhow, I don't care, and he needn't suppose I will. It will be a relief not to have him hanging around any longer."

It might have been a relief, but Anne felt strangely lonely as she walked home alone from prayer meeting the next night. Jerome had not been there. The Warrens were Methodists and Anne rightly guessed that he had gone to the Methodist prayer meeting at Cherry Valley.

"Dancing attendance on Harriet," she said to herself scornfully.

When she got home she looked at her face in the glass more critically than she had done for years. Anne Stockard at her best had never been pretty. When young she had been called "gawky." She was very tall and her figure was lank and angular. She had a long, pale face and dusky hair. Her eyes had been good—a glimmering hazel, large and long-lashed. They were pretty yet, but the crow's feet about them were plainly visible. There were brackets around her mouth too, and her cheeks were hollow. Anne suddenly realized, as she had never realized before, that she had grown old—that her youth was left far behind. She was an old maid, and Harriet Warren was young, and pretty. Anne's long, thin lips suddenly quivered.

"I declare, I'm a worse fool than Jerome," she said angrily.

When Saturday night came Jerome did not. The corner of the big, old-fashioned porch where he usually sat looked bare and lonely. Anne was short with Octavia and boxed the cat's ears and raged at herself. What did she care if Jerome Irving never came again? She could have married him years ago if she had wanted to—everybody knew that!

At sunset she saw a buggy drive past her gate. Even at that distance she recognized Harriet Warren's handsome, high-coloured profile. It was Jerome's new buggy and Jerome was driving. The wheel spokes flashed in the sunlight as they crept up the hill. Perhaps they dazzled Anne's eyes a little; at least, for that or some other reason she dabbed her hand viciously over them as she turned sharply about and went upstairs. Octavia was practising her music lesson in the parlour below and singing in a sweet shrill voice. The hired men were laughing and talking in the yard. Anne slammed down her window and banged her door and then lay down on her bed; she said her head ached.

The Deep Meadows people were amused and made joking remarks to Anne, which she had to take amiably because she had no excuse for resenting them. In reality they stung her pride unendurably. When Jerome had gone she realized that she had no other intimate friend and that she was a very lonely woman whom nobody cared about. One night—it was three weeks afterward—she met Jerome and Harriet squarely. She was walking to church with Octavia, and they were driving in the opposite direction. Jerome had his new buggy and crimson lap robe. His horse's coat shone like satin and had rosettes of crimson on his bridle. Jerome was dressed extremely well and looked quite young, with his round, ruddy, clean-shaven face and clear blue eyes.

Harriet was sitting primly and consciously by his side; she was a very handsome girl with bold eyes and was somewhat overdressed. She wore a big flowery hat and a white lace veil and looked at Anne with a supercilious smile.

Anne felt dowdy and old; she was very pale. Jerome lifted his hat and bowed pleasantly as they drove past. Suddenly Harriet laughed out. Anne did not look back, but her face crimsoned darkly. Was that girl laughing at her?

She trembled with anger and a sharp, hurt feeling. When she got home that night she sat a long while by her window.

Jerome was gone—and he let Harriet Warren laugh at her and he would never come back to her. Well, it did not matter, but she had been a fool. Only it had never occurred to her that Jerome could act so.

"If I'd thought he would I mightn't have been so sharp with him," was as far as she would let herself go even in thought.

When four weeks had elapsed Jerome came over one Saturday night. He was fluttered and anxious, but hid it in a masterly manner.

Anne was taken by surprise. She had not thought he would ever come again, and was off her guard. He had come around the porch corner abruptly as she stood there in the dusk, and she started very perceptibly.

"Good evening, Anne," he said, easily and unblushingly.

Anne choked up. She was very angry, or thought she was. Jerome appeared not to notice her lack of welcome. He sat coolly down in his old place. His heart was beating like a hammer, but Anne did not know that.

"I suppose," she said cuttingly, "that you're on your way down to the bridge. It's almost a pity for you to waste time stopping here at all, any more than you have of late. No doubt Harriet'll be expecting you."

A gleam of satisfaction flashed over Jerome's face. He looked shrewdly at Anne, who was not looking at him, but was staring uncompromisingly out over the poppy beds. A jealous woman always gives herself away. If Anne had been indifferent she would not have given him that slap in the face.

"I dunno's she will," he replied coolly. "I didn't say for sure whether I'd be down tonight or not. It's so long since I had a chat with you I thought I'd drop in for a spell. But of course if I'm not wanted I can go where I will be."

Anne could not get back her self-control. Her nerves were "all strung up," as she would have said. She had a feeling that she was right on the brink of a "scene," but she could not help herself.

"I guess it doesn't matter much what I want," she said stonily. "At any rate, it hasn't seemed that way lately. You don't care, of course. Oh, no! Harriet Warren is all you care about. Well, I wish you joy of her."

Jerome looked puzzled, or pretended to. In reality he was hugging himself with delight.

"I don't just understand you, Anne," he said hesitatingly "You appear to be vexed about something."

"I? Oh, no, I'm not, Mr. Irving. Of course old friends don't count now. Well, I've no doubt new ones will wear just as well."

"If it's about my going to see Harriet," said Jerome easily "I don't see as how it can matter much to you. Goodness knows, you took enough pains to show me you didn't want me. I don't blame you. A woman has a right to please herself, and a man ought to have sense to take his answer and go. I hadn't, and that's where I made my mistake. I don't mean to pester you any more, but we can be real good friends, can't we? I'm sure I'm as much your friend as ever I was."

Now, I hold that this speech of Jerome's, delivered in a cool, matter-of-fact tone, as of a man stating a case with dispassionate fairness, was a masterpiece. It was the last cleverly executed movement of the campaign. If it failed to effect a capitulation, he was a defeated man. But it did not fail.

Anne had got to that point where an excited woman must go mad or cry. Anne cried. She sat flatly down on a chair and burst into tears.

Jerome's hat went one way and his cane another. Jerome himself sprang across the intervening space and dropped into the chair beside Anne. He caught her hand in his and threw his arm boldly around her waist.

"Goodness gracious, Anne! Do you care after all? Tell me that!"

"I don't suppose it matters to you if I do," sobbed Anne. "It hasn't seemed to matter, anyhow."

"Anne, look here! Didn't I come after you for fifteen years? It's you I always have wanted and want yet, if I can get you. I don't care a rap for Harriet Warren or anyone but you. Now that's the truth right out, Anne."

No doubt it was, and Anne was convinced of it. But she had to have her cry out—on Jerome's shoulder—and it soothed her nerves wonderfully. Later on Octavia, slipping noiselessly up the steps in the dusk, saw a sight that transfixed her with astonishment. When she recovered herself she turned and fled wildly around the house, running bump into Sam Mitchell, who was coming across the yard from a twilight conference with the hired men.

"Goodness, Tavy, what's the matter? Y' look 'sif y'd seen a ghost."

Octavia leaned up against the wall in spasms of mirth.

"Oh, Sam," she gasped, "old Jerome Irving and Aunt Anne are sitting round there in the dark on the front porch and he had his arms around her, kissing her! And they never saw nor heard me, no more'n if they were deaf and blind!"

Sam gave a tremendous whistle and then went off into a shout of laughter whose echoes reached even to the gloom of the front porch and the ears of the lovers. But they did not know he was laughing at them and would not have cared if they had. They were too happy for that.

There was a wedding that fall and Anne Stockard was the bride. When she was safely his, Jerome confessed all and was graciously forgiven.

"But it was kind of mean to Harriet," said Anne rebukingly, "to go with her and get her talked about and then drop her as you did. Don't you think so yourself, Jerome?"

Her husband's eyes twinkled.

"Well, hardly that. You see, Harriet's engaged to that Johnson fellow out west. 'Tain't generally known, but I knew it and that's why I picked on her. I thought it probable that she'd be willing enough to flirt with me for a little diversion, even if I was old. Harriet's that sort of a girl. And I made up my mind that if that didn't fetch it nothing would and I'd give up for good and all. But it did, didn't it, Anne?"

"I should say so. It was horrid of you, Jerome—but I daresay it's just as well you did or I'd likely never have found out that I couldn't get along without you. I did feel dreadful. Poor Octavia could tell you I was as cross as X. How did you come to think of it, Jerome?"

"A fellow had to do something," said Jerome oracularly, "and I'd have done most anything to get you, Anne, that's a fact. And there it was—courting fifteen years and nothing to show for it. I dunno, though, how I did come to think of it. Guess it was a sort of inspiration. Anyhow, I've got you and that's what I set out to do in the beginning."

Young Si

Mr. Bentley had just driven into the yard with the new summer boarder. Mrs. Bentley and Agnes were peeping at her from behind the parlour curtains with the keen interest that they—shut in by their restricted farm life—always felt in any visitor from the outside world lying beyond their boundary of purple misted hills.

Mrs. Bentley was a plump, rosy-cheeked woman with a motherly smile. Agnes was a fair, slim schoolgirl, as tall as her mother, with a sweet face and a promise of peach blossom prettiness in the years to come. The arrival of a summer boarder was a great event in her quiet life.

"Ain't she pretty?" whispered Mrs. Bentley admiringly, as the girl came slowly up the green slope before the house. "I do hope she's nice. You can generally calculate on men boarders, but girls are doubtful. Preserve me from a cranky boarder! I've had enough of them. I kinder like her looks, though."

Ethel Lennox had paused at the front door as Mrs. Bentley and Agnes came into the hall. Agnes gazed at the stranger with shy, unenvious admiration; the latter stood on the stone step just where the big chestnut by the door cast flickering gleams and shadows over her dress and shining hair.

She was tall, and gowned in some simple white material that fell about her in graceful folds. She wore a cluster of pale pink roses at her belt, and a big, picturesque white hat shaded her face and the glossy, clinging masses of her red hair—hair that was neither auburn nor chestnut but simply red. Nor would anyone have wished it otherwise, having once seen that glorious mass, with all its wonderful possibilities of rippling luxuriance.

Her complexion was of that perfect, waxen whiteness that goes with burnished red hair and the darkest of dilated violet eyes. Her delicately chiselled features wore what might have been a somewhat too decided impress of spirit and independence, had it not been for the sweet mouth, red and dimpled and curving, that parted in a slow, charming smile as Mrs. Bentley came forward with her kindly welcome.

"You must be real tired, Miss Lennox. It's a long drive from the train down here. Agnes, show Miss Lennox up to her room, and tea will be ready when you come down."

Agnes came forward with the shy grace that always won friends for her, and the two girls went slowly up the broad, old-fashioned staircase, while Mrs. Bentley bustled away to bring in the tea and put a goblet of damask roses on the table.

"She looks like a picture, doesn't she, John?" she said to her husband. "I never saw such a face—and that hair too. Would you have believed red hair could be so handsome? She seems real friendly—none of your stuck-up fine ladies! I've had all I want of them, I can tell you!"

"Sh—sh—sh!" said Mr. Bentley warningly, as Ethel Lennox came in with her arm about Agnes.

She looked even more lovely without her hat, with the soft red tendrils of hair lying on her forehead. Mrs. Bentley sent a telegraphic message of admiration across the table to her husband, who was helping the cold tongue and feeling his way to a conversation.

"You'll find it pretty quiet here, Miss Lennox. We're plain folks and there ain't much going and coming. Maybe you don't mind that, though?"

"I like it. When one has been teaching school all the year in a noisy city, quiet seems the one thing to be desired. Besides, I like to fancy myself something of an artist. I paint and sketch a little when I have time, and Miss Courtland, who was here last summer, said I could not find a more suitable spot. So I came because I knew that mackerel fishing was carried on along the shore, and I would have a chance to study character among the fishermen."

"Well, the shore ain't far away, and it's pretty—though maybe us folks here don't appreciate it rightly, being as we're so used to it. Strangers are always going crazy over its 'picturesqueness,' as they call it. As for 'character,' I reckon you'll find all you want of that among the Pointers; anyway, I never seed such critters as they be. When you get tired of painting, maybe you can amuse yourself trying to get to the bottom of our mystery."

"Oh, have you a mystery? How interesting!"

"Yes, a mystery—a mystery," repeated Mr. Bentley solemnly, "that nobody hain't been able to solve so far. I've give it up—so has everyone else. Maybe you'll have better luck."

"But what is it?"

"The mystery," said Mr. Bentley dramatically, "is—Young Si. He's the mystery. Last spring, just when the herring struck in, a young chap suddenly appeared at the Point. He appeared—from what corner of the globe nobody hain't ever been able to make out. He bought a boat and a shanty down at my shore and went into a sort of mackerel partnership with Snuffy Curtis—Snuffy supplying the experience and this young fellow the cash, I reckon. Snuffy's as poor as Job's turkey; it was a windfall for him. And there he's fished all summer."

"But his name—Young Si?"

"Well, of course, that isn't it. He did give himself out as Brown, but nobody believes that's his handle—sounds unnatteral here. He bought his establishment from 'old Si,' who used to fish down there and was a mysterious old critter in a way too. So when this young fellow stepped in from goodness knows where, some of the Pointers christened him Young Si for a joke, and he never gets anything else. Doesn't seem to mind it. He's a moody, keep-to-himself sort of chap. Yet he ain't unpopular along shore, I believe. Snuffy was telling me they like him real well, considering his unsociableness. Anyways, he's as handsome a chap as I ever seed, and well eddicated too. He ain't none of your ordinary fishermen. Some of us kind of think he's a runaway—got into some scrape or another, maybe, and is skulking around here to keep out of jail. But wife here won't give in to that."

"No, I never will," said Mrs. Bentley firmly. "Young Si comes here often for milk and butter, and he's a perfect gentleman. Nobody'll ever convince me that he has done anything to be ashamed of, whatever's his reason for wasting his life down there at that shore."

"He ain't wasting his life," chuckled Mr. Bentley. "He's making money, Young Si is, though he don't seem to care about that a mite. This has been a big year for mackerel, and he's smart. If he didn't know much when he begun, he's ahead of Snuffy now. And as for work, I never saw his beat. He seems possessed. Up afore sunrise every blessed morning and never in bed till midnight, and just slaving away all between time. I said to him t'other day, says I: 'Young Si, you'll have to let up on this sort of thing and take a rest. You can't stand it. You're not a Pointer. Pointers can stand anything, but it'll kill you.'

"He give one of them bitter laughs of his. Says he: 'It's no difference if it does. Nobody'll care,' and off he walks, sulky like. There's something about Young Si I can't understand," concluded Mr. Bentley.

Ethel Lennox was interested. A melancholy, mysterious hero in a setting of silver-rimmed sand hills and wide blue sweeps of ocean was something that ought to lend piquancy to her vacation.

"I should like to see this prince in disguise," she said. "It all sounds very romantic."

"I'll take you to the shore after tea if you'd like," said Agnes eagerly. "Si's just splendid," she continued in a confidential aside as they rose from the table. "Pa doesn't half like him because he thinks there's something queer about him. But I do. He's a gentleman, as Ma says. I don't believe he's done anything wrong."

Ethel Lennox sauntered out into the orchard to wait for Agnes. She sat down under an apple tree and began to read, but soon the book slipped from her hands and the beautiful head leaned back against the grey, lichened trunk of the old tree. The sweet mouth drooped wistfully. There was a sad, far-away look in the violet eyes. The face was not that of a happy girl, so thought Agnes as she came down the apple tree avenue.

But how pretty she is! she thought. Won't the folks around here stare at her! They always do at our boarders, but we've never had one like her.

Ethel sprang up. "I had no idea you would be here so soon," she said brightly. "Just wait till I get my hat."

When she came out they started off, and presently found themselves walking down a grassy, deep-rutted lane that ran through mown hay fields, green with their rich aftergrowth, and sheets of pale ripening oats and golden-green wheat, until it lost itself in the rolling sand hills at the foot of the slope.

Beyond the sand hills stretched the shining expanse of the ocean, of the faint, bleached blue of hot August seas, and reaching out into a horizon laced with long trails of pinkish cloud. Numberless fishing boats dotted the shimmering reaches.

"That furthest-off boat is Young Si's," said Agnes. "He always goes to that particular spot."

"Is he really all your father says?" asked Miss Lennox curiously.

"Indeed, he is. He isn't any more like the rest of the shore men than you are. He's queer, of course. I don't believe he's happy. It seems to me he's worrying over something, but I'm sure it is nothing wrong. Here we are," she added, as they passed the sand hills and came out on the long, level beach.

To their left the shore curved around in a semi-circle of dazzling whiteness; at their right stood a small grey fish-house.

"That's Young Si's place," said Agnes. "He lives there night and day. Wouldn't it make anyone melancholy? No wonder he's mysterious. I'm going to get his spyglass. He told me I might always use it."

She pushed open the door and entered, followed by Ethel. The interior was rough but clean. It was a small room, lighted by one tiny window looking out on the water. In one corner a rough ladder led up to the loft above. The bare lathed walls were hung with fishing jackets, nets, mackerel lines and other shore appurtenances. A little stove bore a kettle and a frying pan. A low board table was strewn with dishes and the cold remnants of a hasty repast; benches were placed along the walls. A fat, bewhiskered kitten, looking as if it were cut out of black velvet, was dozing on the window sill.

"This is Young Si's cat," explained Agnes, patting the creature, which purred joyously and opened its sleepy green eyes. "It's the only thing he cares for, I believe. Witch! Witch! How are you, Witch? Well, here's the spyglass. Let's go out and have a look. Si's catching mackerel," announced Agnes a few minutes later, after she had scrutinized each boat in turn, "and he won't be in for an hour yet. If you like, we have time for a walk up the shore."

The sun slipped lower and lower in the creamy sky, leaving a trail of sparkles that ran across the water and lost itself in the west. Sea gulls soared and dipped, and tiny "sand peeps" flitted along the beach. Just as the red rim of the sun dipped in the purpling sea, the boats began to come in.

"Most of them will go around to the Point," explained Agnes, with a contemptuous sweep of her hand towards a long headland running out before them. "They belong there and they're a rough crowd. You don't catch Young Si associating with the Pointers. There, he's getting up sail. We'll just have time to get back before he comes in."

They hurried back across the dampening sand as the sun disappeared, leaving a fiery spot behind him. The shore was no longer quiet and deserted. The little spot where the fishing house stood had suddenly started into life. Roughly clad boys were running hither and thither, carrying fish or water. The boats were hauled up on the skids. A couple of shaggy old tars, who had strolled over from the Point to hear about Young Si's catch, were smoking their pipes at the corner of his shanty. A mellow afterlight was shining over sea and shore. The whole scene delighted Ethel's artist eyes.

Agnes nudged her companion.

"There! If you want to see Young Si," she whispered, pointing to the skids, where a busy figure was discernible in a large boat, "that's him, with his back to us, in the cream-coloured boat. He's counting out mackerel. If you go over to that platform behind him, you'll get a good look when he turns around. I'm going to coax a mackerel out of that stingy old Snuffy, if I can."

She tripped off, and Ethel walked slowly over to the boats. The men stared at her in open-mouthed admiration as she passed them and walked out on the platform behind Young Si. There was no one near the two. The others were all assembled around Snuffy's boat. Young Si was throwing out the mackerel with marvellous rapidity, but at the sound of a footstep behind him he turned and straightened up his tall form. They stood face to face.

"Miles!"

"Ethel!"

Young Si staggered back against the mast, letting two silvery bloaters slip through his hands overboard. His handsome, sunburned face was very white.

Ethel Lennox turned abruptly and silently and walked swiftly across the sand. Agnes felt her arm touched, and turned to see Ethel standing, pale and erect, beside her.

"Let us go home," said the latter unsteadily. "It is very damp here—I feel chilled."

"Oh, dear!" exclaimed Agnes penitently. "I ought to have told you to bring a shawl. It is always damp on the shore after sunset. Here, Snuffy, give me my mackerel. Thank you. I'm ready now, Miss Lennox."

They reached the lane before Agnes remembered to ask the question Ethel dreaded.

"Oh, did you see Young Si? And what do you think of him?"

Ethel turned her face away and answered with studied carelessness. "He seems to be quite a superior fisherman so far as I could see in the dim light. It was very dusky there, you know. Let us walk a little faster. My shoes are quite wet."

When they reached home, Miss Lennox excused herself on the plea of weariness and went straight to her room.

Back at the shore Young Si had recovered himself and stooped again to his work. His face was set and expressionless. A dull red burned in each bronzed cheek. He threw out the mackerel mechanically, but his hands trembled.

Snuffy strolled over to the boat. "See that handsome girl, Si?" he asked lazily. "One of the Bentleys' boarders, I hear. Looks as if she might have stepped out of a picture frame, don't she?"

"We've no time to waste, Curtis," said Young Si harshly, "with all these fish to clean before bedtime. Stop talking and get to work."

Snuffy shrugged his shoulders and obeyed in silence. Young Si was not a person to be trifled with. The catch was large and it was late before they finished. Snuffy surveyed the full barrels complacently.

"Good day's work," he muttered, "but hard—I'm dead beat out. 'Low I'll go to bed. In the name o' goodness, Si, whar be you a-goin' to?"

Young Si had got into a dory and untied it. He made no answer, but rowed out from the shore. Snuffy stared at the dory blankly until it was lost in the gloom.

"Ef that don't beat all!" he ejaculated. "I wonder if Si is in his right senses? He's been actin' quar right along, and now to start off, Lord knows whar, at this hour o' night! I really don't believe it's safe to stay here alone with him."

Snuffy shook his unkempt head dubiously.

Young Si rowed steadily out over the dark waves. An eastern breeze was bringing in a damp sea fog that blurred darkly over the outlines of horizon and shore. The young fisherman found himself alone in a world of water and grey mist. He stopped rowing and leaned forward on his oars.

"To see her here, of all places!" he muttered. "Not a word, scarcely a look, after all this long heartbreak! Well, perhaps it is better so. And yet to know she is so near! How beautiful she is! And I love her more than ever. That is where the sting lies. I thought that in this rough life, amid all these rude associations, where nothing could remind me of her, I might forget. And now—"

He clenched his hands. The mist was all around and about him, creeping, impalpable, phantom-like. The dory rocked gently on the swell. From afar came the low persistent murmur of the ocean.

The next day Ethel Lennox declined to visit Si's shore. Instead she went to the Point and sketched all day. She went again the next day and the next. The Point was the most picturesque part of the shore, she averred, and the "types" among its inhabitants most interesting. Agnes Bentley ceased to suggest another visit to Si's shore. She had a vague perception that her companion did not care to discuss the subject.

At the end of a week Mrs. Bentley remarked: "What in the world can have happened to Young Si? It's a whole week since he was here for milk or butter. He ain't sick, is he?"

Mr. Bentley chuckled amusedly.

"I 'low I can tell you the reason of that. Si's getting his stuff at Walden's now. I saw him going there twice this week. 'Liza Walden's got ahead of you at last, Mary."

"Well, I never did!" said Mrs. Bentley. "Well, Young Si is the first that ever preferred 'Liza Walden's butter to mine. Everyone knows what hers is like. She never works her salt half in. Well, Young Si's welcome to it, I'm sure; I wish him joy of his exchange."

Mrs. Bentley rattled her dishes ominously. It was plain her faith in Young Si had received a severe shock.

Upstairs in her room, Ethel Lennox, with a few undried tears glistening on her cheeks, was writing a letter. Her lips were compressed and her hand trembled:

"I have discovered that it is no use to run away from fate," she wrote. "No matter how hard we try to elude it, and how sure we are that we have succeeded, it will rise and meet us where we least expect it. I came down here tired and worn out, looking for peace and rest—and lo! the most disquieting element of my life is here to confront me.

"I'm going to confess, Helen. 'Open confession is good for the soul,' you know, and I shall treat myself to a good dose while the mood is on.

"You know, of course, that I was once engaged to Miles Lesley. You also know that that engagement was broken last autumn for unexplained reasons. Well, I will tell you all about it and then mail this letter speedily, before I change my mind.

"It is over a year now since Miles and I first became engaged. As you are aware, his family is wealthy, and noted for its exclusiveness. I was a poor school teacher, and you may imagine with what horror his relatives received the news of Miles's attentions to one whom they considered his inferior. Now that I have thought the whole matter over calmly, I scarcely blame them. It must be hard for aristocratic parents who have lavished every care upon a son, and cherished for him the highest hopes, when he turns from the women of his own order to one considered beneath him in station. But I did not view the subject in this light then; and instead of declining his attentions, as I perhaps should have done, I encouraged them—I loved him so dearly, Nell!—and in spite of family opposition, Miles soon openly declared his attachment.

"When his parents found they could not change his purpose, their affection for him forced them into outward acquiescence, but their reluctant condescension was gall and wormwood to me. I saw things only from my own point of view, and was keenly sensitive to their politely concealed disapprobation, and my offended vanity found its victim in Miles. I belonged to the class who admit and resent slights, instead of ignoring them, as do the higher bred, and I thought he would not see those offered to me. I grew cold and formal to him. He was very patient, but his ways were not mine, and my manner puzzled and annoyed him. Our relations soon became strained, and the trifle necessary for an open quarrel was easily supplied.

"One evening I went to a large At Home given by his mother. I knew but few and, as Miles was necessarily busy with his social duties to her guests, I was, after the first hurried greeting, left unattended for a time. Not being accustomed to such functions, I resented this as a covert insult and, in a fit of jealous pique, I blush to own that I took the revenge of a peasant maid and entered into a marked flirtation with Fred Currie, who had paid me some attention before my engagement. When Miles was at liberty to seek me, he found me, to all appearances, quite absorbed in my companion and oblivious of his approach. He turned on his heel and went away, nor did he come near me the rest of the evening.

"I went home angry enough, but so miserable and repentant that if Miles had been his usual patient self when he called the following evening I would have begged his forgiveness. But I had gone too far; his mother was shocked by my gaucherie, and he was humiliated and justly exasperated. We had a short, bitter quarrel. I said a great many foolish, unpardonable things, and finally I threw his ring at him. He gave me a startled look then, in which there was something of contempt, and went away without another word.

"After my anger had passed, I was wretchedly unhappy. I realized how unworthily I had acted, how deeply I loved Miles, and how lonely and empty my life would be without him. But he did not come back, and soon after I learned he had gone away—whither no one knew, but it was supposed abroad. Well, I buried my hopes and tears in secret and went on with my life as people have to do—a life in which I have learned to think, and which, I hope, has made me nobler and better.

"This summer I came here. I heard much about a certain mysterious stranger known as 'Young Si' who was fishing mackerel at this shore. I was very curious. The story sounded romantic, and one evening I went down to see him. I met him face to face and, Helen, it was Miles Lesley!

"For one minute earth, sky and sea reeled around me. The next, I remembered all, and turned and walked away. He did not follow.

"You may be sure that I now religiously avoid that part of the shore. We have never met since, and he has made no effort to see me. He clearly shows that he despises me. Well, I despise myself. I am very unhappy, Nell, and not only on my own account, for I feel that if Miles had never met me, his mother would not now be breaking her heart for her absent boy. My sorrow has taught me to understand hers, and I no longer resent her pride.

"You need hardly be told after this that I leave here in another week. I cannot fabricate a decent excuse to go sooner, or I would."

In the cool twilight Ethel went with Agnes Bentley to mail her letter. As they stopped at the door of the little country store, a young man came around the corner. It was Young Si. He was in his rough fishing suit, with a big herring net trailing over his shoulder, but no disguise could effectually conceal his splendid figure. Agnes sprang forward eagerly.

"Si, where have you been? Why have you never I been up to see us for so long?"

Young Si made no verbal reply. He merely lifted his cap with formal politeness and turned on his heel.

"Well, I never!" exclaimed Agnes, as soon as she recovered her powers of speech. "If that is how Young Si is going to treat his friends! He must have got offended at something. I wonder what it is," she added, her curiosity getting the better of her indignation.

When they came out they saw the solitary figure of Young Si far adown, crossing the dim, lonely shore fields. In the dusk Agnes failed to notice the pallor of her companion's face and the unshed tears in her eyes.

"I've just been down to the Point," said Agnes, coming in one sultry afternoon about a week later, "and Little Ev said as there was no fishing today he'd take us out for that sail tonight if you wanted to go."

Ethel Lennox put her drawing away listlessly. She looked pale and tired. She was going away the next day, and this was to be her last visit to the shore.

About an hour before sunset a boat glided out from the shadow of the Point. In it were Ethel Lennox and Agnes, together with Little Ev, the sandy-haired, undersized Pointer who owned the boat.

The evening was fine, and an off-shore breeze was freshening up rapidly. They did not notice the long, dark bank of livid cloud low in the northwest.

"Isn't this glorious!" exclaimed Ethel. Her hat was straining back from her head and the red rings of her hair were blowing about her face.

Agnes looked about her more anxiously. Wiser in matters of sea and shore than her companion, there were some indications she did not like.

Young Si, who was standing with Snuffy their skids, lowered his spyglass with a start.

"It is Agnes Bentley and—and—that boarder of theirs," he said anxiously, "and they've gone out with Little Ev in that wretched, leaky tub of his. Where are their eyes that they can't see a squall coming up?"

"An' Little Ev don't know as much about managing a boat as a cat!" exclaimed Snuffy excitedly. "Sign 'em to come back."

Si shook his head. "They're too far out. I don't know that the squall will amount to very much. In a good boat, with someone who knew how to manage it, they'd be all right. But with Little Ev—" He began walking restlessly up and down the narrow platform.

The boat was now some distance out. The breeze had stiffened to a slow strong wind and the dull-grey level of the sea was whipped into white-caps.

Agnes bent towards Ethel. "It's getting too rough. I think we'd better go back. I'm afraid we're in for a thunder squall. Look at the clouds."

A long, sullen muttering verified her words.

"Little Ev," she shouted, "we want to go in."

Little Ev, thus recalled to things about him, looked around in alarm. The girls questioned each other with glances of dismay. The sky had grown very black, and the peals of thunder came louder and more continuously. A jagged bolt of lightning hurtled over the horizon. Over land and sea was "the green, malignant light of coming storm."

Little Ev brought the boat's head abruptly round as a few heavy drops of rain fell.

"Ev, the boat is leaking!" shrieked Agnes, above the wind. "The water's coming in!"

"Bail her out then," shouted Ev, struggling with the sail. "There's two cans under the seat. I've got to lower this sail. Bail her out."

"I'll help you," said Ethel.

She was very pale, but her manner was calm. Both girls bailed energetically.

Young Si, watching through the glass, saw them. He dropped it and ran to his boat, white and resolute.

"They've sprung a leak. Here, Curtis, launch the boat. We've got to go out or Ev will drown them."

They shot out from the shore just as the downpour came, blotting out sea and land in one driving sheet of white rain.

"Young Si is coming off for us," said Agnes. "We'll be all right if he gets here in time. This boat is going to sink, sure."

Little Ev was completely demoralized by fear. The girls bailed unceasingly, but the water gained every minute. Young Si was none too soon.

"Jump, Ev!" he shouted as his boat shot alongside. "Jump for your life!"

He dragged Ethel Lennox in as he spoke. Agnes sprang from one boat to the other like a cat, and Little Ev jumped just as a thunderous crash seemed to burst above them and air and sky were filled with blue flame.

The danger was past, for the squall had few difficulties for Si and Snuffy. When they reached the shore, Agnes, who had quite recovered from her fright, tucked her dripping skirts about her and announced her determination to go straight home with Snuffy.

"I can't get any wetter than I am," she said cheerfully. "I'll send Pa down in the buggy for Miss Lennox. Light the fire in your shanty, Si, and let her get dry. I'll be as quick as I can."

Si picked Ethel up in his strong arms and carried her into the fish-house. He placed her on one of the low benches and hurriedly began to kindle a fire. Ethel sat up dazedly and pushed back the dripping masses of her bright hair. Young Si turned and looked down at her with a passionate light in his eyes. She put out her cold, wet hands wistfully.

"Oh, Miles!" she whispered.

Outside, the wind shook the frail building and tore the shuddering sea to pieces. The rain poured down. It was already settling in for a night of storm. But, inside, Young Si's fire was casting cheery flames over the rude room, and Young Si himself was kneeling by Ethel Lennox with his arm about her and her head on his broad shoulder. There were happy tears in her eyes and her voice quivered as she said, "Miles, can you forgive me? If you knew how bitterly I have repented—"

"Never speak of the past again, my sweet. In my lonely days and nights down here by the sea, I have forgotten all but my love."

"Miles, how did you come here? I thought you were in Europe."

"I did travel at first. I came down here by chance, and resolved to cut myself utterly adrift from my old life and see if I could not forget you. I was not very successful." He smiled down into her eyes. "And you were going away tomorrow. How perilously near we have been to not meeting! But how are we going to explain all this to our friends along shore?"

"I think we had better not explain it at all. I will go away tomorrow, as I intended, and you can quietly follow soon. Let 'Young Si' remain the mystery he has always been."

"That will be best—decidedly so. They would never understand if we did tell them. And I daresay they would be very much disappointed to find I was not a murderer or a forger or something of that sort. They have always credited me with an evil past. And you and I will go back to our own world, Ethel. You will be welcome there now, sweet—my family, too, have learned a lesson, and will do anything to promote my happiness."

Agnes drove Ethel Lennox to the station next day. The fierce wind that had swept over land and sea seemed to have blown away all the hazy vapours and oppressive heats in the air, and the morning dawned as clear and fresh as if the sad old earth with all her passionate tears had cleansed herself from sin and stain and come forth radiantly pure and sweet. Ethel bubbled over with joyousness. Agnes wondered at the change in her.

"Good-bye, Miss Lennox," she said wistfully. "You'll come back to see us some time again, won't you?"

"Perhaps," smiled Ethel, "and if not, Agnes, you must come and see me. Some day I may tell you a secret."

About a week later Young Si suddenly vanished, and his disappearance was a nine-day's talk along shore. His departure was as mysterious as his advent. It leaked out that he had quietly disposed of his boat and shanty to Snuffy Curtis, sent his mackerel off and, that done, slipped from the Pointers' lives, never more to re-enter them.

Little Ev was the last of the Pointers to see him tramping along the road to the station in the dusk of the autumn twilight. And the next morning Agnes Bentley, going out of doors before the others, found on the doorstep a basket containing a small, vociferous black kitten with a card attached to its neck. On it was written: "Will Agnes please befriend Witch in memory of Young Si?"

www.ingramcontent.com/pod-product-compliance
Lightning Source LLC
LaVergne TN
LVHW040102080526
838202LV00045B/3749